A young man,
a father and
an artist's brush

Living with
Edwin

Curtis Dickman

MVHL

Quantity sales special discounts are available on quantity purchases by corporations, associations, and others. For details, contact the publisher at carol@markvictorhansenlibrary.com

Orders by U.S. trade bookstores and wholesalers. Email: carol@markvictorhansenlibrary.com

Creative contribution by Lyn South
Cover Design - Low & Joe Creative, Brea, CA 92821
Book Layout - DBree, StoneBear Design

Manufactured and printed in the United States of America distributed globally by markvictorhansenlibrary.com

MVHL

New York | Los Angeles | London | Sydney

ISBN: 979-8-88581-021-0 Hardcover
ISBN: 979-8-88581-022-7 Paperback
ISBN: 979-8-88581-023-4 eBook

Library of Congress Control Number: 2022904025

Dedicated to my father Edwin, my children Zander, Rachel and Jacob, and future generations.

With love and appreciation.

ACKNOWLEDGEMENTS

I am grateful to the following individuals for their inspiration, encouragement, and contributions to this book: my wife Celeste, my children Zander, Rachel and Jacob, Dr Mark Victor Hansen, Crystal Dwyer-Hansen, Mark Donnelly, Chrissy Donnelly, Jimmy Walker, Marilyn Murray, Sue Powers MS, Linda Hirsch PhD, Karen Godwin MD, Carol McManus, David Katz, James Hebets, Sara O'Meara and Yvonne Fedderson.

REVIEW

Abuse can leave scars on the body and spirit that last a lifetime, but at Childhelp we see heroic children and brave survivors beat the odds every day and break cycles of abuse. Art therapy is one of the tools we use to help children tell their stories and it is with great enthusiasm that we recommend *Living with Edwin* by Dr. Curtis Dickman, a young boy's journey through the shadows of abuse and into the light of self-reflection using the bright colors of his painting talent to heal. While Dr. Dickman is a world renowned neurosurgeon, it is the exploration of his own mind and mental health that brings this book alive. As a longtime supporter and board member of Childhelp, the author not only shares how to cope with PTSD and find comfort in faith-placing God first which is the key to healing-he challenges the reader to reach out and help others as the final step of recovery. If you are on a path towards finding peace in creativity and service, *Living with Edwin* paints a picture of hope.

Sara O'Meara and Yvonne Fedderson
Founders of Childhelp

CONTENTS

INTRODUCTION

In the beginning, Eisig Dickman begat Samuel who begat Edwin who begat me, Curtis, the middle child of three in a Jewish family in New York City. Ours was a family descended from Russian immigrants, but nationality, culture, and religion weren't the only things passed down from father to son: Physical and emotional abuse perpetrated by one generation on the next was a painful legacy that spanned more than one hundred years in our family history. It's a bitter inheritance I vowed not to pass on to my own children.

I used to believe breaking the generational chain of abusive behavior was impossible. I spent years hiding in substances to mask the pain—as did my mother, brother, and sister, although our "drugs of choice" often differed. It was easier to escape the emotional roller coaster of a husband and father who could be loving one minute and capriciously cruel and destructive the next than to face it. It's a familiar story shared by millions of abuse survivors around the world who live with Post Traumatic Stress Disorder (PTSD) every day.

You may be wondering how my family's story differs from these millions of others, and what value you may find as you read these pages. First, I believe there is power in every story. Inspiration, encouragement, and learning are found in the authentic sharing of universal wounds, and the faith and perseverance required to not only survive the initial trauma, but to rise up and move beyond it.

Second, another legacy passed down from my father to me is the power of art—painting it, not just viewing it—was a powerful therapeutic tool for my father even after he became blind from degenerative eye disease. Painting has been equally cathartic for me in my own journey to healing.

The paintings that Edwin created while blind *(Figures 1-3)* and the therapeutic paintings I created after Edwin died, are located together starting on page 77 in the center of this book.

I'm sharing my story with you—the story of *Living with Edwin* and finding healing in art—to hopefully offer some inspiration and encouragement for your own path as you walk with me for a while. We're all travelers on this road together, and sharing our stories helps make the journey a little less arduous.

Curtis Dickman

July 2022

CHAPTER 1

My father, Edwin Dickman, was born to Samuel and Minna Dickman, in Manhattan, New York, on November 7, 1928. Years before his birth, Edwin's grandparents emigrated from Russia to escape persecution from a violent wave of anti-Semitism from the pogroms. Edwin was their first-born son and, five years later, they welcomed another son, Stanley.

Sam was a dentist, a career path that Edwin would follow years later, and Minna stayed home with the children. The family were devastated when both boys were diagnosed with a medical condition, they inherited from their mother called X-linked Hereditary Choroidal Degeneration, or Choroideremia. This eye disease impairs the blood supply to the choroid, the layer between the sclera and the retina; it causes slowly progressive blindness. During childhood and adolescence, Edwin's vision loss was moderate and he wore glasses to compensate.

Initially, only Edwin's peripheral and night vision were impaired during childhood, but it was enough to impact his ability to play sports like baseball because he wasn't able to detect the position of the ball until it was in the center of his visual field. His poor performance and eyeglasses fueled the taunts and bullying of other children at school and in his neighborhood.

His father, Samuel, had the same hot temper and harsh disciplinarian parenting style that his own father, Eisig had. Sam, intolerant of his children's misbehavior, would often treat Edwin cruelly, lashing him with verbal abuse and brutal physical beatings, often with a belt.

While any physical scars from the abuse would eventually fade, the deep emotional pain and resentment caused by his father were seared into young Edwin's heart where he tried to lock the pain away and ignore it. Because, after all, in those days, boys were told "big boys don't cry"—and this damaging perspective still influences how young boys are raised in our culture today. Between the physical abuse, peer bullying, and degenerative eye disease, there was a lot weighing on young Edwin's shoulders.

By his teenage years, Edwin grew taller and stronger than his father, so the beatings gradually stopped. His torment at the hands of the boys at Stuyvesant High School, however, did not. Eddie was bullied for everything from being Jewish, to being chubby and unathletic to wearing thick glasses and having the last name Dickman (you can imagine the verbal assaults on him as others made derogatory interpretations of his name).

Most of the time, he ignored the taunts and withdrew from social situations with his classmates. When it became too much, and he reached a breaking point, Edwin retaliated in anger against the unrelenting bullying by lashing out physically and got into fistfights.

This time of my father's childhood left a mark on Edwin's life. These emotional wounds, and their effects, would surface again for Edwin later in life. These "emotional abscesses" would later contaminate Edwin's relationships with his wife and children. The bullied child grew up and became a bully to his family. The abused became the abuser.

AUGUST 1956

Edwin met the beautiful Judith Boyer at the Forest Hills Jewish Community Center

Judy and Edwin had a lot in common. They were both second generation Americans, their grandparents having all been Jewish immigrants from the same part of the Ukraine. They were both young professionals; Judy worked in advertising; Edwin had a solo dental practice. They shared similar interests in reading, dancing, traveling, watching basketball, and listening to big band music and jazz.

Judy was voluptuous and witty with long, flaming red hair. They were instantly enamored with one another; one might say it was "love at first sight", but—in reality—it was more like "love at first bite". They escaped the crowded noisy venue of the community center and went to a Chinese restaurant to be alone.

They married in a whirlwind six weeks after they met and honeymooned in the Catskill Mountains at a hotel owned by Edwin's grandparents, Eisig and Jenny Dickman. Judy became pregnant during the honeymoon, but it wasn't the only change to their relationship. Edwin's hot temper reared its ugly head shortly after the wedding. When Judy was four months pregnant, Edwin pushed her during an argument, and she fell down a flight of stairs, fracturing her ankle, clavicle, and several ribs. Edwin was remorseful, apologetic, and insisted that he never intended to hurt Judy. Judy was worried that the fall had injured their unborn child. However, after her fractures healed, she eventually forgave Edwin for injuring her. This was the beginning of Judith's long term role enabling Edwin's cruelty and abuse. They established their roles as abuser and victim very early in their marriage.

It would later come to light that each of them had not been entirely truthful with their beloved before the wedding: Judy, upon discovering Edwin was 28 years old—three years younger than she—told Edwin that she was also the same age. Edwin's secret was much darker and more dangerous: He not only withheld his impaired vision, and impending blindness, from his new bride, he also hid a previous marriage to a woman named Shirley. The marriage was annulled after he beat and choked Shirley, giving her a black eye, and making her fear for her life.

My father's slow, inexorable march to blindness was a time bomb that would eventually explode, and he struggled as he prepared for the eventual blindness that would come. From an early age, my siblings—older brother, Andrew, and baby sister, Dana and I were strictly instructed by our parents to never discuss dad's progressive eye disease to anyone under any circumstances. A shroud of secrecy, mistrust, and fear of disclosure were always with us. Edwin's condition became the Big Family Secret, the Dickman Curse.

The family vow of silence was absolute, and we were intimidated into that silence by our parents with threats of homelessness and bankruptcy. It became our family doctrine: It's us against the world. The five of us were united in our desperation and fear. This world view created a state of emotional, social, and physical isolation. Both of my parents worked excessively and had only a few superficial friendships. Most times, they avoided social interactions. When in public, Edwin gently held Judy's elbow when walking so she could discretely guide him without anyone suspecting his vision was poor.

My parents focused their energy on preparing for the economic fallout that would come when dad would be blind and no longer able to work. For all their financial preparation, they ignored the emotional crises that loomed large on the horizon. Both parents were consumed with preparing for disaster which left little energy for their children or each other.

As Edwin's vision continued to decline, and he inched ever closer to losing his dental practice and total dependency on others for his every need, he became an emotional pressure cooker that regularly boiled over with devastating rage as he became increasingly desperate in his never-ending battle against fate. He was the quintessential Dr. Jekyll and

Mr. Hyde. There were days where Edwin was calm, rational, patient and loving. And there were raging, abusive, lunatic Edwin days that came without warning.

CHAPTER 2

When I was very young, Edwin was larger than life to me. I adored him unconditionally. He was gentle and loving. Powerful and strong. Smart, funny, and warm. In a nutshell, he was the center of my universe. Sunday mornings were my favorite time. Dad didn't go to work and while my siblings still slept, I would crawl into my parents' king-size bed and make a Curtis Sandwich by snuggling between them. It was a beautiful, sweet moment of exclusive time and affection with my parents.

It was during one of these Sunday mornings that he explained his eyesight was slowly deteriorating and, someday, he would be completely blind. I couldn't understand how—or why—this terrible thing could happen to my daddy, and all I wanted to do was fix him. I would often close my eyes and pretend that I could never open them again. I walked around the house, eyes tightly shut, bumping into walls and furniture. The exercise frightened me, and it made me sad because there was nothing, I could do to fix daddy's eyes.

I developed profound empathy and compassion for my dad's suffering, and it eventually became my primary motivation to become a physician and, eventually, a neurosurgeon. My father's condition, while extremely painful for our family, inspired me to heal people. It's most certainly a "silver linings" kind of perspective, and a gift for which I will always be thankful.

Summer 1964. I was five years old. I remember our family vacation and there was an Olympic-sized swimming pool at the hotel. Dad taught me to swim during that vacation. I would climb on his back for submarine rides up and down the length of the pool.

"Dive, dive, dive!" Edwin said before submerging his body just below the water's surface and breast stroking his way across the pool.

Exhilarated, I kept my head above the cool, clear water as we swam together. It was the most delightful experience, a feeling of bliss and peace that I vividly remember to this day. I had dad all to myself. There was nothing like being in the water with him, laughing and playing. We were bonded and I felt so safe in his arms. The water has calmed and soothed me from that day onward.

***

The first eight years of my life were relatively carefree and happy. As children, when we were disrespectful or disobedient, my father would use his hand or a belt to spank my siblings and me—older brother Andrew and younger sister, Dana. At the time, I didn't know corporal punishment was child abuse—as children, we don't know the way our parents raised us may not be healthy—but I remember being terrified each time it happened.

One day, when I was five, something happened that upset daddy. I don't even remember what it was, but he was furious with me.

"Curtis, you're worthless. I hate you and will never talk to you again,' he yelled in his rage. He stormed off leaving me shattered and devastated. He ignored me for days. Refused to speak to me, or even acknowledge my presence, despite my repeated pleas for forgiveness. I was overwhelmed by grief and pain. My father had rejected me, and it seemed like it would never end.

Because he was the center of my universe, I unquestioningly believed he was right, as most children of this age do. After all, he was the smartest, strongest man I knew. What had I done to make him treat me this way? I resolved to learn to be good "so *Daddy will love me*".

After a few days, my father began speaking to me again and everything returned to a superficial version of "normal." Except for me. The emotional impact this incident had on me was profound. I began having frequent nightmares and fears of a monster under my bed that would hurt me *(Figure 4)*. I feared that I would do something to make Daddy angry again and he would again make me feel defective and unlovable. I buried these emotional wounds as deeply in my subconscious as I could; it was all too painful to bear. I call this wound "Zeus's injury."

Even so, the wound pain and trauma still seeped into my life, manifesting as hypersensitivity to rejection, and feelings of being inadequate, defective, and unlovable. I was frequently anxious and developed panic attacks. Later in life, these subconscious fears would become a motivator for success—as the drive to prove myself grew. They would also become my Achilles' Heel, impacting my relationships and my life at the deepest levels.

***

When I was eight years old, Edwin's behavior started to become more abusive toward my mother, Judy. He yelled and cursed at her. On occasion, he even hit her. Andy, Dana, and I had never before seen him this violent. Although infrequent, the assaults on Mom terrified us. The house was filled with fear and anxiety. I learned that I could protect my mom by stepping in between my parents and acting as a human shield. When I was small, this was an effective temporary deterrent to keep my father from hurting Mom. As I grew older, he would assault me, too, whenever, I tried to intervene or protect her from his rage.

When things got bad, my mom would put Andy, Dana, and me in the car and take off. We would stop at the nearest Chinese food restaurant—food was mom's addiction, and Chinese food helped soothe her. Then, we would stay at a hotel for a few days to, in Mom's words, "teach daddy a lesson." I was my mom's rescuer during these crises, which increased in frequency and intensity as Edwin's vision got worse.

Even as I became mom's rescuer against my father's growing attacks, I was still relentlessly motivated by a desire for validation and attention from them both. My attempts to be the helpful child . . .the worker, doer, rescuer, and healer—distinguished me from my brother Andy—who was often lazy and docile—and my cute, but unmotivated, younger sister Dana. I became the one my parents relied on for chores, errands, and any other support they needed.

***

Eyesight problems in my family did not stop with Edwin. My brother, Andy, developed issues with his vision around age four, but they were unrelated to Edwin's progressive hereditary eye disease. He wore eyeglasses at an early age, but an incident when he was ten years old changed everything: A boy forcefully struck Andy on the back of the head with a book just after he stepped off the school bus. Andy immediately went blind.

My parents panicked and immediately took him to the emergency room. The hospital ophthalmologist diagnosed Andy with detached retinas in both eyes, with extensive eye damage. Andy's vision was filled with floaters: large, dark, floating spots that left him unable to read and struggling to discern objects forms and shapes. The assault on Andy, and his subsequent blindness, created an epic crisis for our family which only served to heighten the anxiety, anger, and fear we felt about Edwin's impending blindness.

My parents took Andy to the Eye and Ear Infirmary at Harvard Medical School in Boston. There, a renowned ophthalmologist and retinal specialist, Dr. Harold Freeman, performed a pioneering experimental surgery to reattach

Andy's injured retinas. It was one of the first operations of its kind on a child. Over the next year, Dr. Freeman performed several successful surgeries on Andy, although the procedures left him with large holes, or blind spots, in his visual field. His vision was permanently impaired, requiring him to wear thick "coke bottle" glasses so he could read. He sustained poor night vision and was restricted from participation in contact sports to prevent recurrent retinal detachment.

During the surgeries, Edwin temporarily shut down his dental practice. My parents and Andy moved to Boston while Dana and I stayed home with Grandpa Sam and Nana Minna. While the surgeries were considered successful, the swing of a schoolbook radically, instantaneously changed our lives forever. Andrew's blindness was a dreaded premonition of the future when Edwin would eventually go blind. It amplified everyone's emotions and paranoia and set the stage for the progressive emotional unraveling that occurred over the next eight years. It was like pouring gasoline onto our emotional firestorm.

JULY 1972

When I was 11, my father urged Andy and me to join the boy scouts. He thought that they would teach me great values and principles that were important for our development. Andy and I love playing outdoors, so we joined immediately. We had lots of camping trips, earned badges, and learned to be more self-reliant. During our first summer as Boy Scouts, Andy and I went to Ten Mile River Scout Camp, the same camp our dad attended thirty years prior. We were scheduled to be there for an entire month.

Before this, I had only been on a few short camping trips. I was scared when I found out we were going to a sleep-away camp, but it helped a little bit to know that I was going with Andy. We shared a tent and helped each other out. We had each other's backs. Despite his impaired vision, Andy flourished at camp. My experience was very different.

I was too scared, homesick, and uncomfortable to enjoy this time at summer camp. In reality, I was still afraid of monsters under the bed, at this age, and in the aftermath of Andy's attack I developed a deep mistrust of strangers, and a fear of more emotional and physical harm. Being away from the familiar surroundings of home, fanned the flames of these fears and more anxiety.

Before the end of the first week, I wrote my parents a letter saying how much I hated it because of all the "downsides"— like mosquito bites, poison ivy, diarrhea, and lousy food. An excuse, of course, because I couldn't admit to my real fears. In the end, my letter writing campaign paid off. After only a week at camp, my parents came to get me. Andy stayed the additional three weeks and had a blast.

The next summer, I wanted to attend a Boy Scout camp closer to home, but Andy wanted to go back to Ten Mile River again. So, I went to Baiting Hollow Scout Camp. This experience would prove to be even more disastrous than the previous year's camp experience. When I arrived at camp, I felt abandoned by Edwin and Judy. I felt scared, alone, and exposed. I was terrified of being hurt again after Andy's attack. I didn't know who to trust—everyone seemed like a possible threat. I was a frightened, mistrustful twelve-year-old boy.

Within an hour of arriving at camp, I met two older teenage boys at my campsite. They started bullying me and taunting me about my last name. I begged them to stop, then threatened to hit them. One of the boys snuck behind me and got down on his knees, while the second boy pushed me backward. I fell onto my back with a resounding thud. It was humiliating and I was enraged. Even though I wasn't physically injured, my ego was bruised. The abuse didn't stop there.

The boys called me names, laughed at me, and threatened to beat the living daylights out of me if I didn't "watch myself." I was devastated; this felt like confirmation from the outside world of my defectiveness, inadequacy, and unlovable status. I panicked. I desperately wanted to escape. While I could escape from threats of being beaten up again, I couldn't run from the demons lurking in my subconscious. These feelings of inadequacy and incompetence would follow me wherever I went.

I went to the camp nurse's cabin and faked illness. I told her that I had a sore throat, muscle aches, and fatigue. It was enough to convince her to keep me quarantined in a comfortable bed in the cabin for twenty-four hours. When the nurse took my temperature for the first time, it registered as 98.6, normal. It was an old-school glass thermometer, the kind with silver liquid mercury inside. Glass thermometer readings can be impacted with externally applied heat, so it was an easy thing to manipulate, if you knew how to do it. When the nurse took my temperature the second time, she left me alone with the thermometer for a few minutes.

As I sat there, a light bulb went off in my head. I suddenly understood how to rig the thermometer so it would read a falsely high temperature. I grasped the bulbous grey tip between my thumb and index finger and snapped my wrist and arm, causing the mercury to miraculously rise above normal. When the nurse returned, my temperature was a raging 104 degrees.

I was ecstatic. This was my ticket home. Judy and Edwin were summoned to the camp and took me to Smithtown General Hospital where my pediatrician admitted me for observation and a diagnostic workup. The admitting diagnoses was a Fever of Unknown Origin, also called an FUO. My parents were so concerned, they lavished me with affection and attention. They even joked with me, calling me their little alien because I had a "UFO".

I stayed in the hospital for 3 days. One or both of my parents sat by my bedside most of the time, only leaving to go to work or go home to change clothes or sleep. Since the temperature manipulation strategy worked so well at camp, I decided to continue the practice in the hospital, intermittently recreating my fever using the same technique that I had discovered. I fixed the thermometer only when there was no medical staff in the room. I needed to provide evidence to the doctors and my parents that I was ill enough to stay out of Boy Scout camp, but not seriously ill.

After several days, my temperature magically returned to normal, as did all my lab tests. The doctor discharged me from the hospital, but I still complained that I didn't feel well, so my parents allowed me to come home rather than return to camp. Munchausen Syndrome* is the diagnoses used by psychiatrists for the fabricating illnesses the way that I did as a child. To me, this was a clever little escape hatch for my emotional demons, and it brought the added bonus of my parents rescuing me from camp and showering me with their love and attention.

Years later, I would use a similar tactic to manage—or rather, mismanage—the intolerable trauma wounds in my psyche that I didn't know how to handle, but with more serious and risky consequences.

***

Emotional coping mechanisms come in all sizes and shapes; my mother coped with her wounds with food. Judy's entire universe revolved around consuming food, and at the center of her gastronomic galaxy was Chinese food. She knew

---

*Footnote: Wikipedia definition: **Munchausen syndrome** is a psychiatric factitious disorder wherein those affected feign disease, illness, or psychological trauma to draw attention, sympathy, or reassurance to themselves. It is also sometimes known as hospital addiction syndrome, thick chart syndrome, or hospital hopper syndrome. True Munchausen syndrome fits within the subclass of factitious disorder with predominantly physical signs and symptoms, but they also have a history of recurrent hospitalization, travelling, and dramatic, untrue, and extremely improbable tales of their past experiences.

the location and quality rating of every Chinese restaurant within a 50-mile radius of our house. On the night she and Edwin first met, they ate at the same Chinese restaurant twice.

Judy ate Chinese food when she was happy. She ate it when she was sad. Sometimes she ate Chinese food for no reason at all, other than she loved the taste. Her food obsession, however, extended far beyond Chinese cuisine. She loved to cook and eat just about everything. Jewish holiday meals were filled with traditional chopped liver, gefilte fish, brisket, potato pancakes, and matzo ball soup. On New Year's Eve, the tradition was a homemade Spanish Paella filled with seafood, sausage, and chicken with a fragrant sofrito sauce and saffron rice.

As a result of chronic and compulsive overeating, coupled with zero physical exercise, my parents became obese and developed numerous obesity related illnesses—diabetes, hypertension, arthritis, and congestive heart failure. Edwin successfully battles his obesity. After developing Type 2 diabetes, he lost one-hundred pounds on Weight Watchers. Judy, however, waged a mock war with her obesity; one in which she frequently waved the white flag of surrender to temptation. She was always dieting but cheated and impulsively indulged in sweets and Chinese food. She never overcame her chronic obesity.

As a result of my parents' food addictions, the entire family struggled with unhealthy eating habits, especially with the habit of self-medicating emotional distress with comfort foods. I struggled for most of my life to maintain a healthy weight and, fortunately, have been relatively successful. My siblings, Andy and Dana, were different. They were chubby as pre-teens, overweight as adolescents, and morbidly obese as adults. Obesity became the mechanism of self-destruction for Judy, Andy, and Dana. They would all commit slow, painful suicide, one bite at a time.

CHAPTER 3

"Judith, you have diarrhea of the mouth and constipation of the brain," Edwin said to my mother, one night during dinner. He was in a mood, one that employed sarcasm and it put all of us in a mood, too. If you looked hard enough, you could see the eggshells strewn across the dining room floor, just waiting for one misstep to crush them to pieces and trigger my dad into another rage.

I learned at an early age that no one in my family fought fair; none of us knew how to express the genuinely uncomfortable emotions of irritation, anger, disappointment, or frustration in healthy ways. Edwin was the worst bully in the family, but everyone else engaged in dysfunctional behavior to meet emotional needs, too. Emotional manipulation and sarcasm were the primary weapons, especially when they felt angry. The first manifestation was my father's bizarre rejection of me when I was five years old, and it continued for years.

Edwin regularly employed sarcasm to express anger, disappointment, or frustration. He would berate my mother, condescending statements—like the diarrhea and constipation statement. Sometimes, the sarcastic jabs were delivered with a mockingly humorous tone, but we all knew there was nothing funny about the intent of these passive aggressive words.

***

When I was a child, most of Edwin's expressions of dysfunction were at a subliminal level. However, as I approached adolescence—which coincided with my father's rapidly deteriorating vision—Edwin's emotional turmoil began building up even more, like steam in a pressure cooker. The built-up pressure finally exploded and scalded the entire family. No one was left unscarred. His bullying intensified and became overwhelming.

It's often said you only hurt the ones you love. This is primarily true because we know the sensitive underbellies and weaknesses of the ones closest to us, their Achilles' Heels, so to speak. Everyone in my family used these individual sensitivities as tactical assault targets to gain the emotional advantage during conflict. Going for the jugular became the best way to win any argument. However, the winner prevailed at the emotional expense of the loser. Our battles were vicious. The goal: inflict the most pain and humiliation on one's opponent. We didn't realize that this was a dysfunctional, losing proposition for everyone involved; nobody won these arguments. Not really. We all lost something in the process.

The ammunition we employed spanned a spectrum of emotional and physical abusiveness: cursing, spitting, hitting, betrayal, and blackmail. Nothing was out of bounds and outright cruelty was often the order of the day. Edwin was the primary role model for this behavior, but everyone followed his example to varying degrees. We didn't recognize the destructiveness of our family dynamics.

I grew wary of disclosing my vulnerabilities and secrets to my parents and siblings, knowing that anything I said could be used as a weapon against me later when everything hit the fan. I longed to trust my family, but the frequent attacks and betrayals left me feeling constantly on guard and emotionally unsafe. *(Figure 5 & 6)*. I was hypervigilant for the next emotional or physical assault. The bullying generated a myriad of painful, destructive feelings for all of us: resentment, distrust, anxiety, and poor self-esteem. These feelings left us constantly angry and disappointed, filled with self-doubt, contempt, and fear as we isolated ourselves from one another. As mentioned before, this paranoia extended to people outside the family, too.

One poignant example of bullying by the entire family is what I call my Potato Salad Trauma. It happened when I was nine years old. Mom made potato salad for dinner one night. I had never eaten it before. Even though I loved eating other kinds of potatoes—French fries and baked potatoes, for example—and loved mayonnaise on sandwiches or tuna, I just didn't find the idea of potatoes mixed with mayonnaise particularly appealing. I refused to eat any of it, convinced I would hate it.

"Just try one bite," Mom pleaded. "I know you'll like it."

"Eat the potato salad, Curtis,' my father said, casting a menacing glance in my direction. "Your mother went to a lot of trouble making dinner. The least you can do is eat it."

"I don't want to," I whined. "It looks gross."

The harder they tried to convince me, the more adamantly I refused. We went back and forth over that potato salad, and the anger escalated. Andy and Dana took my parents' side and, suddenly, it was four against one. I was cornered. Frightened. Angry. I dug my heels in.

"No! You can't force me to eat it, and I won't," I yelled.

Edwin jumped up from his chair, his face red with anger. "I'm going to force you to eat the goddamned potato salad, and you're going to like it, no matter what!"

My mother and siblings all rallied behind him. I was petrified because he sounded and acted like he was serious. I didn't believe he would, or could, force me to eat the potato salad. I certainly knew he could never force me to enjoy it, and I had already made up my mind that I wasn't going to like it.

The situation turned surreal and literally scared the living daylights out of me. My father snatched me from the dinner table, threw me down on to the living room floor, and pinned me down beneath his massive bulk.

I panicked, overwhelmed by fear as I struggled against my father.

"Please don't, dad," I cried, begging him to stop. My heart pounded, my skin flushed, and my stomach did flip-flops. I felt helpless. Angry. Betrayed and disgusted. No matter how much I pleaded, the assault continued.

My father pried my mouth open by jabbing his thumbs into the middle of my cheeks. It was excruciating. My mother, meanwhile, scooped a heaping forkful of the hated potato salad into my mouth as my brother and sister stood watching and cheering them on. My father then forced my mouth closed and demanded that I chew and swallowed the food.

I couldn't breathe. Edwin's hand covered both my mouth and my nose. I felt like I would suffocate. He insisted that I chew and swallow. "I'm not going to let you move or breath until you swallow that food," he said.

I was helpless. I truly feared for my life, so I did as I was told. What happened next was both tragic and beautiful. As soon as I swallowed the potato salad, a tsunami of nausea hit me. My stomach, filled with my partially digested dinner, convulsed and I spewed its entire contents—including the hated potato salad—like an eruption of Mount Vesuvius. Within seconds, my parents and siblings were covered in vomit.

Even though it was an involuntary reaction for my body to reject the forcefully fed food, I was delighted with the outcome. It felt like my body had fulfilled a vengeance quest because my mind was numb and reeling. I couldn't have consciously formulated such a perfect plan of revenge against my abusers.

After Edwin released his hold on me, I discovered that the stress of the physical attack caused me to wet myself. As my family struggled to clean themselves, and the living room, I escaped upstairs and took a shower, brushed my teeth, and went to bed.

I tried to forget this insane incident, but I've never been able to escape the pain and aftereffects of the attack. *(Figure 4)* I was horribly emotionally scarred by the incident, and, to this day, potato salad is one of my emotional triggers. I was conditioned, like one of Pavlov's dogs, and I can't even think of potato salad without developing severe nausea and the desire to vomit. The thought of, or smell of, potato salad conjures the devastating fear, desperation, and helplessness in that situation and my visceral response to the memory is overwhelming nausea.

CHAPTER 4

E scaping my family when everything blew up became the most important strategy in my emotional survival plan. It became easier to accomplish when I was 13 years old, and my parents turned our unfinished basement into my bedroom. I was ecstatic. Sharing a room with then 15-year-old Andy was a literal disaster.

My brother was a quintessential teenage slob. He was Oscar Madison of the "Odd Couple" to my Felix Unger. Only worse and without the laugh track. Andy's messes disgusted me. The room was strewn with empty food containers, dirty plates and utensils, chicken bones, stinky socks and more. Not to mention, he had a nasty habit of jerking off beneath the covers of his bed while reading *Penthouse* magazine whether I was in the room or not. Gross! I couldn't live that way anymore and still maintain what little emotional equilibrium I possessed.

The basement bedroom was the perfect refuge from everything painful in my world. The space was bright with white paneled wood walls, red trim and red baseboards, and a checkered linoleum floor. I could keep it in immaculate condition. And it was entirely mine, a safe space with a lockable door away from the loony bin. Whenever things got too heated upstairs, I could isolate myself from the chaos, and self-medicate with loud Rock and Roll music.

My passion was Deep Purple, Led Zeppelin, Bad Company, the Rolling Stones, the Eagles, the Doobie Brothers, and other hard rock bands of the 70s. I loved music so much that I learned to play the guitar and tenor saxophone; I fantasized about becoming a rock star, being adored by fans, and effortlessly getting laid all the time.

My room was large enough for my rock band to practice without feeling crowded. It was awesome. I was happy and extremely relieved to be segregated from "the loony bin" in the house above me.

The room had another kind of escape hatch, too. A hinged window that opened outward to provide an escape route in case of fire, which allowed me to easily sneak out of the house undetected. I could also welcome friends to visit without my parent's knowledge. There was a fan which vented the room to the outside, which facilitated smoking. It was a juvenile delinquent's paradise.

My teenage defiance enraged Edwin. Because he couldn't see or navigate well enough to chase after me, I could escape his fury, and the beatings, by running from him. But my rebellion came with a price.

"You can't catch me, man," I would taunt him, mocking his weaknesses to his face. "I'm too fast and you can't even see me, can you?"

Seething, Edwin would glare at me then retrieve the electric guitars from my room and smash them to pieces right in front of me on our front porch. When he calmed down, and the guilt kicked in, he would eventually help pay for a new guitar which only slightly lessened my resentment toward him. We were caught in a never-ending cycle of abuse.

The pain was too much for me to bear, so I numbed myself with denial, avoidance, escape and self-medication. The perpetual chaos and abuse at home created unbearable feelings, so I had to banish them from my mind. It was the only way I could cope.

I survived by stuffing all the painful feelings deep inside my subconscious, compartmentalizing them in a box, locking them up, and throwing away the key, beyond my conscious awareness and recognition. Retreating to the basement was my emotional modus operandi, for my survival and self-preservation.

Music wasn't the only thing I used to dull the anguish in my life. One night, while attending a school sponsored roller-skating field trip on a Friday night, I thought I would show my friends how cool I was. I broke into my parent's liquor cabinet and stole a bottle of *Cold Duck* left over from Andy's Bar Mitzvah. I knew they would never detect the missing bottle because my parents rarely drank alcohol. I had once half emptied one of their vodka bottles and refilled it with water; they never knew the difference. I was 13 years old.

My pals and I met on the darkened football field and stole several sips of the sweet, sparkling wine. When we finished, we corked the half-full bottle, and hid it behind the field goal post. After we returned from roller skating, I salvaged the bottle and locked it up in my school locker to save for future use and promptly forgot about it.

The following Monday, just before lunchtime, I was summoned out of my wood shop class by the school's vice principal. Mr. Cassidy had a wrestler's physique and a "speak softly but carry a big stick" philosophy toward the students under his charge. He was well known for spanking the more aggressive boys with a thick wooden paddle he kept in his office. His paddle served as an effective deterrent to brawling for many students.

I was a naïve kid. I had no clue why Mr. Cassidy wanted to talk to me, but the fact that he had pulled me from class meant he wasn't interested in a casual chat.

"Curtis, how is it going at home?" He asked as we walked through the crowded lunchroom. His tone was gentle and friendly. I almost wanted to trust him. "Any problems you want to talk about?"

But I couldn't tell him the truth. I couldn't talk about Edwin's rapidly deteriorating vision or the way he stuffed potato salad down my throat as a kid or smashed my guitars when he was angry. I couldn't talk about the pain and the chaos. Our family secrets required absolute silence.

"Nope," I answered, avoiding eye contact. "Home is ok."

"Are you sure? Maybe you're having trouble with your classes or homework, then."

"No," I shrugged. "School is ok."

We walked upstairs to the second floor of the school. As we approached my locker, I was struck with a thunderbolt of sudden recognition. *The bottle of wine was still in there.*

My stomach knotted in an ominous pit of anxiety, and adrenaline surged through me.

"Is there anything you want to tell me, Curtis, before I ask you to open your locker?" Mr. Cassidy asked. "Any contraband in there?"

My heart continued to race, and I felt dizzy. The most prominent sensation felt like an electric shock deep within my midsection that pierced me to the core. I knew there was no way out of it.

"Nothing but a half-drunk bottle of Cold Duck," I replied with a sheepish expression.

"Ok. Open it up, please."

Mr. Cassidy marched me to his office and called my parents. Being sentenced to a 7 day in-school suspension, where I would be isolated in the school library to study alone, was the least traumatic part of the entire experience. The real pain came after Edwin and Judy picked me up from school. They were furious.

We didn't immediately go home. Instead, they took me to a barber shop and insisted I get a crew cut; their version of a punishment that would fit my crime. I had long hair at the time, and they knew I loved it. So, they took what I valued most and squeezed that pressure point. Knowing the punishment could be exponentially worse, I reluctantly agreed. I wore a ski cap to school for the next two months to hide my "Scarlet

Letter" branding, the visible symbols of my transgression and my imperfection according to my parents.

The emotional armor I wore had its chinks; I was hypersensitive to being seen as a delinquent or perceived as an outsider, different from other "normal" teens. I remember the fear and humiliation I felt when my parents found out about my little escapade. It felt like the whole world was crashing down on me. *(Figure 6)*

On the outside, it seemed that I had quickly recovered from the episode and moved on, presumably wiser for the correction of my parents. But, as with most abuse, it would create an important backdrop that would influence future events in my life. Little did I know that only two years after this incident I would face a similar, but more devastating punishment at the hands of my parents.

FEBRUARY 1974.
SMITHTOWN HOSPITAL, NEW YORK

I sat next to the hospital bed in the Intensive Care Unit as my mother, Judy, lay comatose. Filled with despair and fear, I held her cold, still hand as the ventilator methodically pumped air in and out of her lungs. The cardiac monitor beeped in a slow methodic rhythm as the machine breathed for her. A tangle of catheters and drain tubes protruded from every orifice and penetrated her skin.

My mother appeared to be dying. My entire world was crumbling before my 14-year-old eyes.

I am Jewish and even though I celebrated my Bar Mitzvah the year before, I doubted whether God existed. I had never seen Him. Never spoke to or felt him, or ever really prayed. As someone who believed in logic, I was confused.

The concept of God felt as fabricated as the emperor's new clothes. "How can I believe in something I can't see? Something that can't be observed. How can I accept what everyone else seems to take at face value and just...have faith?" I wondered.

On this gloomy day, as my mother lay near death, I was desperate to try anything. As I gently stroked Judy's forehead, pushing her short, red hair out of her eyes, I prayed. "Please don't let my mother die. If you save her life, it will confirm to me that you're real, and I will believe in you forever."

I sat beside her, crying, and praying for hours. "Please, God, help me. Please, God, answer, my prayers. Save my mom." Finally, exhausted, I fell asleep at her bedside.

My mother had attempted suicide, and I blamed Edwin. In fact, I did more than blame him. I despised him. His vision was rapidly deteriorating, and he was close to being blind and unable to work. Unable to cope with the situation, his abusive tantrums had recently escalated. The emotional intimidation and physical beatings increased in frequency and severity.

The night before mom's suicide attempt, my father exploded at the dinner table. Andy, Dana, and I were all present to witness the explosion. I don't remember what triggered him, but he began screaming and cursing at Mom. In a violent rage, he even overturned the dinner table, sending food, dinnerware, and our bodies flying in different directions. It felt like a bomb had exploded.

I thought my dad had finally snapped and feared he would kill us all. Edwin's vicious tirade continued, and he went to the china cabinet. He grabbed the gold-plated heirloom china my mother inherited from her mother and threw it onto the backyard patio, shattering the china into millions of pieces. He deliberately, mercilessly destroyed part of my mother's cherished family legacy.

As Dad destroyed the china, Mom, Andy, Dana, and I ran from the house without stopping to grab any belongings. We left in our Rambler station wagon with the clothes on our backs, grateful we were still alive and sustained minimal physical injuries. We were, of course, all in shock; the psychological fallout was devastating. This was the worst episode of physical and emotional terror we had ever encountered with Edwin.

Mom drove us to the nearest Chinese restaurant. How we were able to eat with the fear and adrenaline coursing in our veins, I don't know, but my mother soothed us with steaming hot wonton soup, egg rolls, sweet and sour pork, and mounds of fried rice. As the adrenaline began to dissipate, we checked into a hotel room with two double beds. Dana and Mom shared one bed while Andy and I shared the other.

At one point, Andy whispered that he had some powerful reefer, so we went out for a walk and got stoned. As we got high, we talked about how Edwin needed to be locked in a padded room because he was obviously insane. We talked of running away from home permanently. Along with the weed, the discussion served to numb our agony as well. Andy and I were comrades, partners in protecting each other and our mother and sister.

Mom was distraught and exhausted from the ordeal. She fell asleep in her clothes. I gently removed her shoes and socks and kissed the top of her head as I covered her with a blanket. As I lay down to sleep, I fervently hoped, as I had when my hair was shorn, that the entire thing was just a bad dream.

***

The next morning, mom sneaked us back into the house while Dad was at work in the dental office next door. We rushed to collect some clothes and personal items, then went back to the hotel. Mom was irritable and sullen. Dark circles beneath her eyes made it clear she was physically and emotionally drained.

Later that afternoon, Andy and Dana went out to a movie while I stayed at the hotel to keep Mom company. I fell asleep while watching an episode of Gilligan's Island. I awoke to a sudden, urgent shake of my shoulders.

"Curtis, help me," my mother cried, slurring her words. Even though I was disoriented and groggy, I knew my mother's nearly incoherent state meant something was seriously wrong.

"Mom, what happened?" I asked, as I jumped out of bed.

"I don't know. Pills," she said. "I want the torment to stop. I just want it all to stop. I'm so tired."

I ran to the bathroom and found empty pill bottles in the garbage. Valium. Phenobarbital. Elavil. My mother had swallowed every pill. I grabbed the empty bottles to take them with us.

"Help me, Curtis," she begged tearfully, swaying on her feet like a drunken sailor. "Help me."

I tried to calm my nerves. I struggled to get Mom out of the hotel and down to our old gray station wagon. She could barely walk. I settled her into the passenger's seat and got behind the wheel. I didn't yet have my driver's license, but I had occasionally driven my parent's car around the block. I started the car and took off for Smithtown General Hospital.

It was afternoon rush hour, and the roads were congested. Fueled by adrenaline, I drove as fast as I could, occasionally driving on the shoulder of the highway to bypass stalled traffic. I didn't care if the police pulled me over; all I could think about was saving my mom. As we drove, my mom's eyes closed, and her head limply rolled forward. A moment later, she vomited into her lap. I stepped on the gas.

It took 30 minutes to get to the hospital, but it seemed like an eternity to me. Mom was comatose by the time we arrived at the emergency room. I was overwhelmed. I thought she was dying.

As the medical staff whisked her through the double glass sliding doors into the ER, I tried to follow but the security guard blocked me.

"Please, let me go with my mom. She needs me,' I begged.

"Let the doctors and nurses do their job, son," he replied. "She's in the best hands."

"But—"

"I'm sorry, son, but you need to sit in the waiting room until they're able to come and talk to you."

Numb and dizzy, I waited for hours in the waiting room. Finally, a nurse appeared and told me that Mom was alive, but on a ventilator and in critical condition. They were admitting her to the ICU, and I could see her after she was put in the room. It was nearly ten o'clock at night before I was allowed to see her, 6 hours after we arrived at the hospital.

My father never visited Mom during her hospitalization. His response when I called him from the hospital was a complete shock. I dialed the phone in Mom's room with trembling fingers.

"Hello," Edwin growled into the phone.

"Dad, it's Curtis."

'Where the hell are you, boy? Where is your mother?"

"We're at Smithtown Hospital." I felt like vomiting.

"What the hell are you doing there?"

"Mom swallowed a lot of pills. She's in a coma. They have her on a ventilator." I paused, my rage and fear stuck in my throat. "Dad, can you come, please? We need you."

"Why should I come to the hospital?" Dad sneered. "Your mother is so inept; she can't even pull off committing suicide."

"So," I stammered, not quite believing my ears. "You're really not coming?"

"No, I'm not coming. You're on your own," he said. Then, the line went dead.

He abandoned us. I was my mom's sole rescuer and caretaker. I felt the weight of the world on my young shoulders and a burning rage toward my father.

I stayed by her bedside, leaving only to go to the bathroom. The nurses brought me meals.

Two days later, Mom woke up and her ventilator and breathing tube were removed. The doctors said it was a miracle she survived. It was a miracle any of us survived Edwin. I was utterly exhausted from the four-day ordeal of running a physical, emotional, and spiritual gauntlet.

The hospital social worker contacted my father and arranged for him to come to the hospital. Mom and Dad met with the social workers and with a psychiatrist. They agreed to begin counseling.

Upon discharge from the hospital, Mom returned home. She and dad engaged in limited individual therapy, as well as couples counseling, but none of it satisfactorily addressed or resolved their emotional issues. Eventually, we warily reunited as a family, though we remained distrustful and fearful of Edwin. We never knew when his next episode of explosive, irrational rage would occur. We lived in a perpetual emotional minefield.

We didn't realize that our family's torment and suffering were only just beginning. What we found in the days after Mom's suicide attempt—in this temporary eye of the emotional hurricane—was only the beginning.

One of the many lessons I learned as my mother lay near death, was the value of prayer and faith. God had answered my prayers. He had my back when I needed Him. And it was an experience that would lead me on a journey of faith for the rest of my life. *(Figure 7)*

CHAPTER 5

B y the time I was a 15-year-old high school sophomore, the crew-cut punishment for having stolen alcohol in my school locker, had been safely stowed away in my subconscious. My hair had long since recovered and was shoulder-length at this point. It fit perfectly with my dreams of being a rock god, the next "Jimmy Hendrix".

I still played the guitar, tenor sax, and sang in several different rock bands. My love for music soon became more than just a way of escaping my crazy family, hanging out with new friends, and making out with the high school groupies my bands managed to garner. My identity was defined in my Rock Star Wannabe image. My long hair and rugged appearance represented my defiance of authority, and the rejection of my parent's values. It established my own identity separate from their grown-up nerdy, "square", clean cut images.

My long hair was a sacred part of this identity, and it bonded me with my peers. My view of my hair was analogous to that of Biblical hero, Samson. Like him, my hair was my source of strength, social identity, autonomy, and power. As a teenager, I primarily hung out with other stoner and rocker kids who were—for the most part—good-natured and relatively normal. The exception Greg, my next-door neighbor.

A year younger than me, Greg was a scrawny little sociopathic juvenile delinquent. His parents were divorced, and his older brother was a heroin addict. My neighbors were not exactly the "Brady Bunch". Greg followed in his brother's footsteps and used any drugs he could get his hands on, once set the local woods on fire just for kicks, and sought out perverse, bizarre adventures for the adrenaline rush.

Like I said...sociopathic juvenile delinquent. And I was inexorably drawn to him as a continuous source of adventure.

We built a small clubhouse in his backyard from discarded plywood. We covered the dirt floor with old carpeting, tacked on a tar paper roof, and installed locks on the small front door to create an emergency retreat when needed. We even ran long extension cords from his house out to the clubhouse, so we'd have electricity. We decorated with posters, black lights, folding chairs, and a mattress.

This was the place where Greg and I snuck away to smoke pot and hash, drank Mad Dog 20/20, and hoped to get laid (although the latter never happened, just a few make out sessions with a few neighborhood girls). We were wild and didn't care. We wanted to live life on our terms. The cost would prove to be more abuse at the hands of my parents.

One of our escapades involved setting off an entire pack of firecrackers on the school bus. Meant to be an amusing practical joke, but our parents and Mr. Cassidy didn't share the opinion. We both were suspended from school for 10 days and endured another month of detention after that. I tried to avoid accountability with my parents.

"I was just along for the ride," I told them. "It was all Greg's idea, and I couldn't stop him. He planned it all, and he's the one who lit the fuse. I'm just so glad no one was hurt by his sick joke."

In truth, I was a co-conspirator; a nervous, but willing participant in "blowing up" the school bus. It was an adrenaline rush, but I meant it when I said I was relieved our practical joke hadn't hurt anyone.

"You're never to see that boy again, Curtis," my father screamed. "Never. You stay away from him."

"Don't disobey us on this, Curtis," my mother warned. "If you do, you'll be severely punished."

They didn't elaborate on the consequences, but I knew they had enough on their plates with work and dealing with my siblings, not to mention the stress of Edwin's rapidly deteriorating vision. I thought they were just blowing smoke up my ass and, after a short period of time with no further repercussions, I ignored their warning and began hanging out with Greg again.

I came home late one weekday after getting high with Greg. Edwin asked me to come to his dental office next door to our home. I was unaware and unprepared for the trap that awaited me. I walked in to find my mother and father holding hair clippers and scissors.

"Thought you could get away with hanging out with the white trash next door, did you?" Edwin asked in a hostile, ominous tone.

"We expressly forbid you from spending time with that boy," my mother said, gripping the shears. "Why didn't you listen?"

"We warned you to stay away from him and you defied us. You're going to pay a heavy price for your disobedience."

Their anger exploded into rage and a brutal, physical assault. They grabbed me and wrestled me to the ground. Edwin punched me repeatedly and restrained my arms. Judy flung her 300-pound body on top of me, crushing my torso. I was instantaneously suffocated both physically and emotionally. Terror, fear, and anxiety overwhelmed me, and the sudden adrenaline surge did nothing to help me defend myself or escape. They had the physical advantage; it was two against one, and I was trapped.

"Oh, my God!" I screamed. "What are you doing? Let me go! Oh, my God, please let me go!"

It was surreal, a nightmare I could never have comprehended me. Edwin pinned me to the ground under his full bodyweight—all 280 pounds of him. Judy, meanwhile, held my head immobile by grabbing fistfuls of hair and my earlobes, making what little movement I could manage painful. Edwin took the scissors and hair clippers and violently chopped my treasured long hair off in large chunks.

"Please, please don't do this," I begged as the insane violation continued. I tried to shake my head free, to kick my body free of them, but I wasn't able to do it. After what seemed like an eternity, they released me. My only thought was to escape, so I ran to my room in the basement and locked the door.

When I finally looked in the mirror, I was aghast. My head was nearly bald with scattered remnants of patchy hair. By cutting off my hair, they tore the fabric of my identity, ripping my heart out of my chest and casting it into an abyss. I was overwhelmed, exhausted, helpless, and angry. So furious that I cried and cursed and cried and cursed and cried some more until I was utterly spent.

I collapsed on the bed and fell into a deep sleep in my dark, quiet room, trying to find relief in the suspended animation of my cocoon. I awoke several hours later, hoping to find it was all just an awful nightmare, a figment of my imagination. A hope quickly dashed when I touched my bald scalp and the scraps of remaining hair that confirmed the horrendous reality.

My heart pounded and my stomach churned as nausea and anxiety overwhelmed me. The feelings and thoughts were too intense to process. I tried to escape and deny what had happened but there was a constant reminder when I looked in the mirror; a bald demon stared back at me. I was adrift on a raft on a sea of helplessness and despair, no lifeguard or life preserver in sight. I wanted to die.

I isolated myself in my basement bedroom, avoided going to school or out in public. I was ashamed and the distrust and paranoia of others—especially my family—only grew in the weeks and months that followed. Self-medication with the strongest weed I could find—Maui Wowie, Panama Red, Thai

Sticks, and Acapulco Gold, and any other top shelf stuff I could find. I became, in the words of the Pink Floyd song, being comfortably numb in the emotional vacuum the pot created. It was soothing and allowed me to avoid the bitterness of my painful reality.

The marijuana served a useful purpose: it enabled me to survive my crippling pain. Without it, I would likely have put a .44 Magnum to my temple and pulled the trigger. A bullet through the brain would have been preferable to my suffering. Thank God I had weed to help me cope with my intolerable suffering. The physical and emotional assault of having my hair chopped off had an immense impact on me because it violated, shattered, really, my identity...my sense of self.

I vowed to myself that I would never betray or hurt my future loved ones. I vowed I would escape my abusive family and the legacy of abuse to start a new life with a new family. I vowed to never abuse or torment my future wife and children, to allow the pathological physical and emotional torture of my parents to be passed on to the next generation. It was important to recognize the massive damage that generational abuse has on subsequent generations, but as a teenager, I became a master of denial and emotional suppression. Pot greased the skids of my psyche and helped me keep the lock box in my mind securely locked. I would later learn that ignoring my trauma, and the resulting PTSD, would routinely jump up to bite me in the ass in adulthood. *(Figure 8-10)*

***

Returning to school one week after my parents shaved my head bald was the last thing I wanted to do, but they forced me. My mind and gut were still reeling from the fallout of my emotional and physical torment. I was ashamed of my naked scalp, which was a glaring beacon of my social and emotional exile for all to see. I was an immediate outcast among my long-haired hippie peers.

Andy knew the torture I had endured, but I begged him not to tell anyone else at school about what happened. I was ashamed of what happened and the change in my appearance that broadcast my defectiveness to the world. My parents shearing my hair off socially, emotionally, and physically emasculated me. I was a raw nerve, hypersensitive, vulnerable, anxious, and paranoid.

The perpetual stares of everyone at school were intolerable, but the treatment only got worse. Kids would tease me, calling me baldie or rubbing my head while saying "I wish I had a monkey." These things may seem relatively benign—the casual teasing of kids that should not be taken to heart—but they were salt rubbed into an open wound, and anxiety, dread, and panic were my constant companions. All my most intense subconscious fears of being hurt and rejected were now my worst nightmares come true.

I felt like a circus freak, and outcast, trapped in a living hell of being teased as a one-man side show. I wanted to run and hide from the whole world. I fantasized about committing suicide but didn't have the nerve to hurt myself. I remembered the feeling of being cared for and nurtured by my parents during the Boy Scout Camp summer when I faked the fever and wound up in the hospital for three days.

Riding my bicycle home from school one day, a spontaneous plan for escaping my pain came to me. I never intended it to reach such an extreme level; I was just along for the ride that my trauma damaged soul concocted an elaborate plan to find some amount of solace from the pain.

I rode on the wrong side of the street as I headed home, in the opposite direction of the scant flow of traffic on the road. An oncoming car approached me as I neared a corner, and came very close to the bike, but did not actually hit me. I fell off my bike onto the street in a dramatic staged accident. I screamed in pain, feigning severe pain in my left knee even though I only had superficial scrapes and bruises from the fall off the bike. It was all an act, and I believed it was the only viable escape route from the torment of my life.

The driver of the car stopped and helped me to the side of the road. I faked being unable to walk and he called my mom, who came and picked me and my bike up. No police or ambulances were ever summoned. Judy took me to the emergency room at St Charles Hospital, where they took x-rays and found no fractures. They wrapped my left knee in an ace bandage and gave me crutches. I continued to feign severe pain in my left knee, and I was unable to walk and stayed home from school.

"Bingo!" I thought. "I've hit the jackpot." No one suspected that my knee injury was faked, and it felt fine.

A week after the accident, I saw an orthopedic surgeon called Harold Massoff. He was friendly and reminded me of a slightly grey, older version of "Hawkeye" Pierce from the television show M*A*S*H. Dr. Massoff made goofy jokes to put me at ease, even called me "Coitus" instead of Curtis, the same nickname my Grandpa Sam called me. I called him Dr. Funny Bone.

There were x-rays done, but no fractures were detected. Because I continued to push the fiction that my pain was persistent and severe with any knee motion or weight-bearing, he was concerned there was internal damage to my knee. He scheduled me for an arthrogram, a diagnostic procedure that injected a contrast dye into the knee to outline the ligaments and joint surfaces. I sweated bullets, my heart raced with fear when the radiologist produced a thick, six-inch long needle to inject the dye into my knee. I briefly considered backing out of the game, however, the radiologist stuck the needle into my knee before I could object further.

When the results came back a week later, Dr. Funny Bone called us into the office and explained that the arthrogram revealed a torn meniscus. The shredded cartilage in my knee was, in his considered opinion, the obvious source of my pain, and he recommended surgery. I never told him that my knee didn't really hurt. Never having had surgery before, I was ignorant about the process and its implications.

"What's the worst that could happen?" I mused. "I'm going to go along with this and see what happens. It sure beats returning to school and facing all that torture." I couldn't bear facing my classmates and surgery seemed perfectly rational and acceptable at the time; just one more escape hatch from my torment.

The evening before the surgery, I was admitted to the hospital and additional pre-operative lab tests were performed. I was anxious, but there was no way I would reveal my scam now. As bizarre and irrational as it seems to be now, especially as a surgeon, it was critical for me to continue the charade, at the time. My emotional survival depended on it.

The morning of the surgery, a technician greeted me in my room and shaved all the hair off my left leg. He then started an IV and administered valium to help me relax. The sedative quickly did its job, and I had a good, relaxed buzz going when they wheeled me into the operating room. Again, I was comfortably numb in my floating world. Even with the sedatives in my system, I vividly took in my surroundings. It all felt like a weird movie that is imprinted into my memory. I remember the chilled, white-walled operating room, the glaring lights and masked nurses and doctor in blue scrubs. I remember the feel of the operating table beneath my body and the thin sheet that covered me.

My veins felt chilled from the IV fluids coursing through them, and I heard the beeps of the cardiac monitor after the EKG leads were attached to my chest. I even remember the sweet smell of ether in the mask as the anesthetist fixed it over my face. Then, I drifted into a swirl of unconsciousness until total blackness took me and there was no more feeling, no more pain, and no more memories.

***

I vaguely remember the recovery room as I came out of sedation. Nurses hovered near me, asking if I was in pain. Their voices were like angels, and their white uniforms enhanced the illusion. I knew the morphine that dripped through the IV into my veins provided pain relief from any intense pain I might be feeling, and it was an intense high. Soon enough, I drifted off into oblivion again.

The next time I woke, I was groggy, and my left knee was on fire. The pain burned and throbbed in continuous, severe waves.

"Oh, my God," I thought. "What have I done?" I had no clue it would be this bad, but I couldn't turn back the clock, the damage could not be undone. Thankfully, the nurses continued to bring regular, generous doses of narcotics—both injectable and oral—which made the pain tolerable.

The postoperative experience was further complicated by my inability to urinate. The nurse palpated my abdomen, gently pushing on my distended bladder and, matter-of-factly informed me that if I didn't pee soon, they would insert a catheter into my penis and drain my urine. This scared the daylights out of me.

"No way in hell is anyone sticking anything into my dick," I vowed. My penis was a source of pleasurable fondling, not a conduit for a garden hose to help me pee. I grabbed a urinal and tried to pee. I pushed and strained for what seemed an eternity, but my bladder would not cooperate. Not even a drop. My knee pain intensified from the desperate, anxious efforts straining to pee.

Finally, before the nurse returned to insert the catheter, I felt a trickle begin and dribbled a weak stream of urine into the urinal. PHEW! It worked. Although it took a long time to drain my bladder, I finally got it done. My reward was another shot of pain medication that allowed me to drift back to sleep, oblivious of any further pain.

Four days later, I was discharged from the hospital with crutches and medical orders that excused me from school attendance for four months. Instead, I had home tutoring. I spent my days doing schoolwork and knee exercises during physical therapy appointments. Most importantly, my hair grew out during this time, and I no longer looked like a circus freak.

***

The postoperative knee pain gradually resolved. While the operation left a long scar on my left knee, the entire debacle also left a massive scar on my psyche; a gaping, open emotional wound that remained unresolved for years. Even so, my latest, and most severe, of my two Munchausen Syndrome scams led to a seminal event in my life: I enrolled in a high school biology course and decided to do an extra credit report for the class on the details of my knee surgery.

Using my father's Gray's Anatomy textbook, I drew pictures of sections of knee anatomy that were relevant to my surgery and wrote a report filled with simple, yet detailed anatomical descriptions of my procedure using the Latin terms. My efforts paid off. I earned an A+ on the report.

It's ironic that my life's calling to become a physician, a healer like Dr. Massoff and my father, Edwin, evolved from my fabricated plot to escape the emotional torment of an abusive family. When I announced my intention to become a doctor, it was met with enormous enthusiasm by my parents.

"This is super," Edwin exclaimed, obviously pleased and proud of my decision. Judy was excited, too, and they both nurtured and encouraged my career path in medicine.

In truth, Dr. Massoff was a role model as well. I put him on a pedestal because he was skilled, revered, trusted, and important. The fact that my parents were obviously excited about my chosen career solidified the desire for similar validation of my worth, lovability, and competence. From the age of 15, I had a singular goal: pursuit of academic excellence and unwavering commitment that would lead me to become a doctor.

My pursuit of my chosen career did not resolve my emotional trauma. While my primitive, self-harming Munchausen strategy worked, temporarily, and led to the epiphany of my true life's calling, it didn't resolve the trauma locked deep in my subconscious. I couldn't hide from those inner demons forever.

***

OCTOBER 1974, CENTRAL ISLIP STATE PSYCHIATRIC HOSPITAL, NEW YORK

I really didn't want to die. I just wanted the pain to stop. Eight months after my mother's suicide attempt, I contemplated slitting my wrists. I. Had no one to trust or turn to. I was abused and tortured by my family. I had no one to talk to and nowhere to go. I was 15 years old, a sophomore in high school. And I was desperate for help.

I didn't have the chutzpah to slit my wrists, so, instead, I took a handful of Judy's Valium and smoked a joint. It made me intensely stoned and drowsy. An hour after taking the pills, I went to my parents. All I really wanted was for someone to listen, to understand and accept me and sooth my overwhelming pain.

"Mom. Dad," I said. "I need help."

They looked up at me and immediately knew I was on something.

"What did you take?" Mom asked.

"Your Valium," I said.

"How much of it did you take?" Dad asked.

"I don't know," I replied.

Mom checked her pill bottle and, after determining it likely wasn't a dangerous or fatal dose, they took me to Central Islip State Psychiatric Hospital rather than to the emergency room. Central Islip was built as an asylum in the 1800s and the outside of the building looks like the stereotypical insane asylums in horror films.

After meeting with the doctors and social workers, they determined I wasn't serious about committing suicide, but was depressed, emotionally overwhelmed, and in serious need of treatment. They also met with my parents and recommended the entire family begin individual and group family therapy.

The staff sent me home, but enrolled me in an intensive psychiatric treatment program for teens at a day hospital. To participate in this program designed to integrate regular classroom work with group and individual therapy, I completely disassociated myself from my stoner friends. My life became a regimented schedule Mondays through Fridays from eight o'clock in the morning until five o'clock in the evening. The schedule consisted of classroom work and talk therapy, along with art and music therapy programs. The program lasted for three months.

After starting treatment at the day hospital, I realized that I wasn't crazy, but I did have severe Post Traumatic Stress disorder (PTSD). While other patients in the program experienced visual or auditory hallucinations, I did not. I was relieved to learn that I wasn't psychotic. The intensive counseling and seclusion of the hospital walked me back from the edge of the mental health crisis cliff. Most importantly, my entire family began intensive outpatient counseling that lasted for several years. It was the beginning of our road to recovery.

All of us participated in twice weekly individual psychotherapy and family therapy under the care of skilled clinical psychologists. The journey was slow, but progressive, and set the stage for healing for years to come. *(Figure 9)*

THE ART

(Figure 1) Heaven Over the Ocean

(Figure 2) West Maui Mountains

(*Figure 3*) Sunset Over Monument Valley

Figures 1-3 were created circa 1978-79 by Edwin Dickman after he developed complete blindness. These three landscape paintings were made with acrylic paints on canvas, based upon his memories when his vision was intact. An art therapist aided Edwin by choosing appropriate colors and orienting him to the canvas.

Water was used symbolically in the beach scene painted by my father in figure 1. Water is an essential element; a basic nourishment for the human spirit which is required to sustain life. Water personally symbolizes the intimate bonds I developed with my father at an early age, our playfulness, joy, love, and affection. Water also symbolizes the womb filled with amniotic fluid, a primordial soup or sea of life. Water symbolizes a source of comfort, buoyancy, cleansing, rebirth, and renewal. Conversely, water can symbolize external threats such as flooding, drowning, a tsunami, etc.

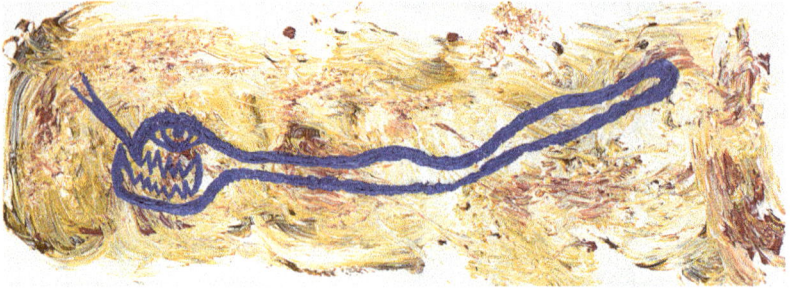

(Figure 4) Bedtime Monsters

This snake was a depiction of the monster under my bed. My therapist observed that it looked like a toothbrush and represented my father, who was a dentist. The background looks like vomit, related to my "Potato salad trauma".

(Figure 5) The Psyche of the Abused Child

(Figure 6) Alone and Hopeless

(Figure 7) Tears From Heaven

This painting represents God looking down from heaven with sadness and compassion for all the pain and suffering in the world. It represents God's desire for us to repair, heal, and transform the world and to correct injustice.

In Judaism the concept of humanity's shared responsibility to heal the world is called Tikkun Olam. (Hebrew:‏סלוע ןוקת or סלוע ןוקית).

This concept originated in the early rabbinic period, was given new meanings in the kabbalah of medieval times, and is a fundamental moral principal in modern Judaism

Another interpretation of this painting is the concept of continuing to be influenced by my father Edwin long after he died. In this painting, Edwin is looking down on me from heaven. His eyes are no longer blind. He has clear vision, perspective, and insight from his healthy beautiful green eye. He is simultaneously crying tears of joy and tears of sadness. His tears of sadness represent his appreciation of my heartache, grief, pain, and suffering. He empathizes with my profound insight and my newfound capability to understand and express all my genuine feelings. His tears of joy represent his appreciation of my life successes, achievements, triumphs, and emotional healing. He validates my humanness, my lovability, my worth, my competence, my spirit, and my soul.

His tears of joy also represent his pride and appreciation for inspiring me to create beautiful, meaningful, heartfelt therapeutic paintings, which have helped me mend my own broken heart and wounded spirit.

The beautiful orange yellow sunrise heralds this new day, this new chapter in our lives. The calm tranquil blue water in the ocean represents the vast deep intimacy Edwin and I shared together. Beginning with our submarine rides together in the pool, extending throughout our lives, water represents Edwin's and my genuine deep mutual love and affection for each other. The tears create waves and ripples in the water which symbolize Edwin's ongoing, reverberating impact on my life and psyche. His presence perpetually resonates in my life, even though he resides in heaven.

(Figure 8) Crucifixion of the Tuna Fish

This painting symbolizes my locked up, deep emotional torment and the fears which arose from the emotional and physical abuse during my childhood and adolescence. I hated the abuse which I encountered and perpetually tried to escape. I endured the abuse of my father and family, and I loved them even though I was wounded, confused, and appalled by their behavior. This painting represents my fears of being eternally bullied, punished, abused, tormented, and persecuted.

The crucified tuna fish is roasting in an emotional hell, nailed to the cross, and has a nail painfully impaled through the eye. The helpless limp tuna fish is sad, suffering, and numb; restrained and in shock; yet is stoically surviving and enduring the pain. The tuna's world is literally turned upside down. The nail through the eye represents the suffering and pain I endured due to my father's blindness and abuse.

The tuna symbolizes me. Tuna fish was my favorite food when I was a child. I loved to eat tuna fish sandwiches so much that my mom Judy used to kid me that she was going to change my middle name and call me Curtis "Tuna Fish" Dickman.

It is paradoxical that I am nailed to a cross in the painting because I am Jewish. The painting symbolizes my prior religious ambivalence and my rejection of Judaism as a teenager. As a teen, I saw documentary movies of the Holocaust which depicted the horrendous torture and murder of Jews in European concentration camps. I was aghast and profoundly frightened by the vivid movie images of starving Jews, mountains of Jewish corpses, mass graves, gas chambers and crematoriums. I was hypersensitive to these images because of my childhood abuse and my preexisting strong fears of persecution, torture, and suffering. As I watched the movie, I felt overwhelmed with fear and thought "If this is what the world does to Jews, then I don't want to be a Jew any longer". I subsequently tried to suppress my Jewish identity and abandoned going to synagogue. As I grew older, I still enjoyed celebrating Jewish holidays with my parents, siblings, wife, and children, and retained an affinity for my cultural heritage. After beginning psychotherapy and confronting my issues later in life, I returned to synagogue with my children, and fully shared my Jewish culture and religion with my children and family.

The nail through the eye also symbolizes the pain my father's blindness caused him, me, and my family.

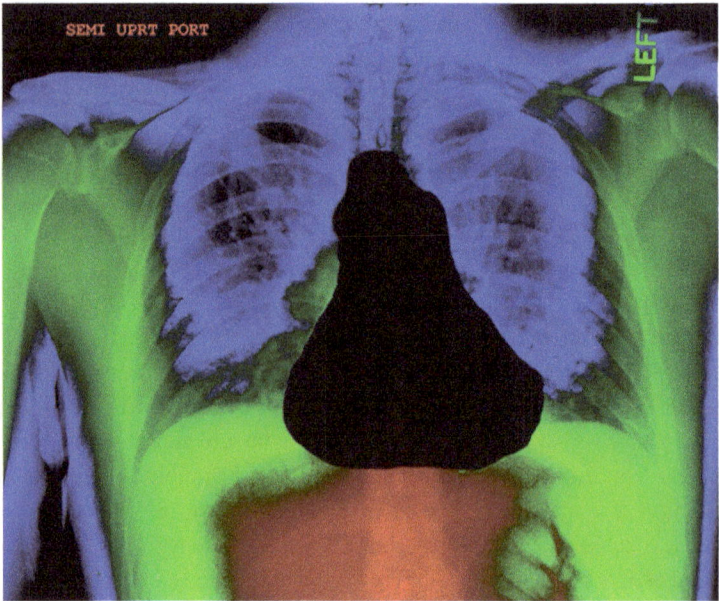

(Figure 9) Unchain My Heart

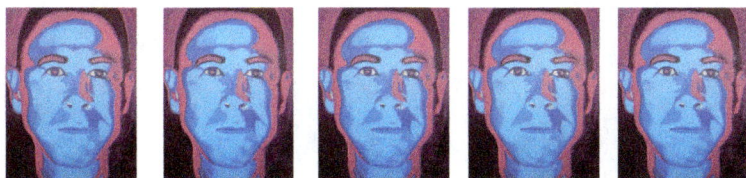

Shock   Anger   Sadness   Resentment   Shame

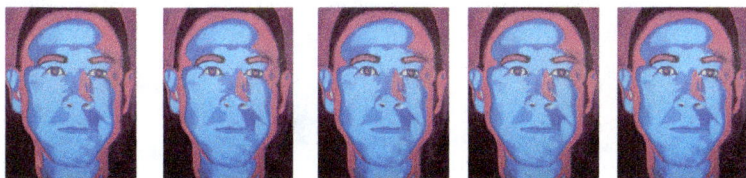

Doubt   Frustration   Dissociation   Fear   Anxiety

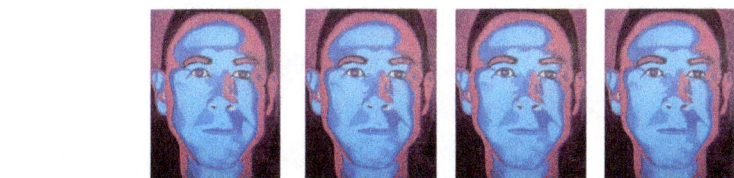

Absent   Guilt   Grief   Panic   Burnout

(Figure 10) The Many Faces of PTSD

(Figure 11) A Bottle in Front of Me or A Frontal Lobotomy?

This painting represents addiction and the destructive process of self-medicating with alcohol or drugs. Painful feelings are difficult to process. Addictions work temporarily to deny or avoid acknowledging painful feelings by numbing the brain and disconnecting the awareness of emotional pain. Self-medicating is an unproductive, unhealthy, destructive coping mechanism which never permits effective acknowledgement or processing of the underlying feelings. The brain is injured by chronic abuse, like having a frontal lobotomy. Meanwhile, the melting Daliesque clock depicts time ticking away, as the anonymous individual avoids the opportunity for emotional healing and recovery.

This painting was inspired by my frustration and heartbreak over my brother and sisters' self-destructive addictions. Andrew and Dana each died prematurely from the combined effects of drug abuse, cigarette smoking, and compulsive eating disorders. I tried to help them but was ineffective; they never fully embraced my attempts to intervene.

(Figure 12) The Thinker

(Figure 13) I Surrender

This painting depicts God reaching down from heaven to rescue me from drowning in my emotional turmoil and life stresses.

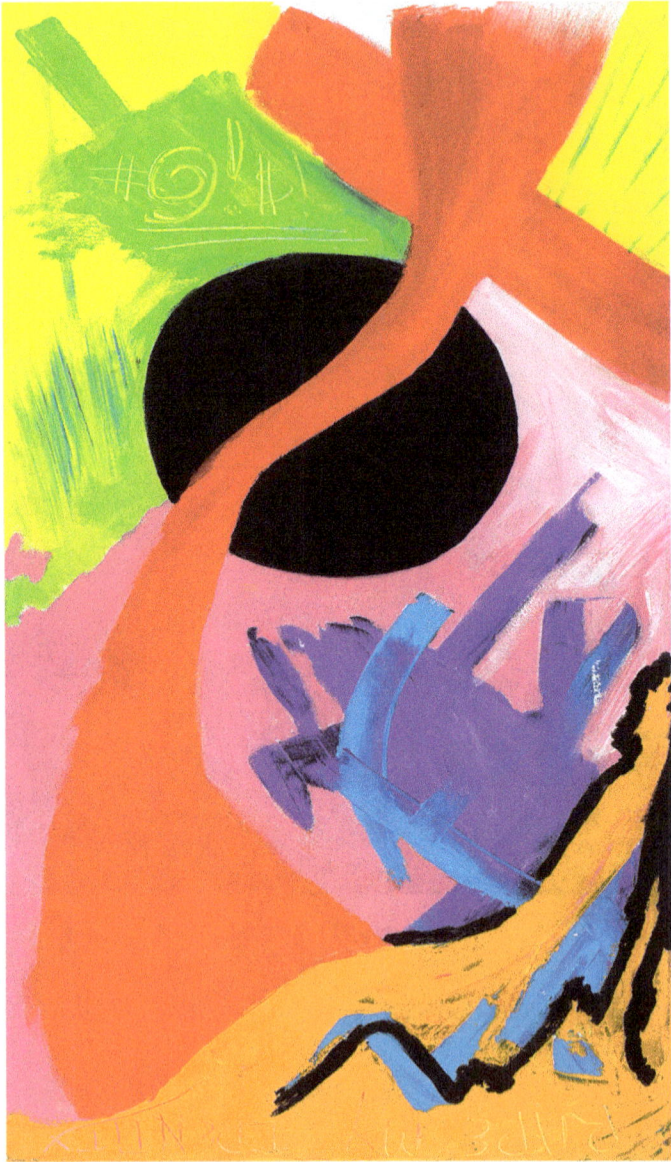

(Figure 14) Rape of Adolescent Innocence

I painted this cathartic piece while I listened to loud Led Zeppelin music. I painted rapidly, from my "gut", using palate knives and acrylic paints. The painting was deeply emotional, emanating from my subconscious, unlike the meticulously planned and laboriously executed technical paintings which I previously painted. I was not assigned a particular topic or subject matter, but was instructed to crank up the music loudly, spontaneously paint "from the heart" and "see what happens".

The results astounded me and provided plenty of material to discuss in my therapy. My painting portrayed a dramatic episode of torture and abuse which my parents inflicted upon me when I was a teenager. My feelings and thoughts were screaming to be released from my subconscious, where I had kept my painful memories of this devastating trauma locked away for decades. I had not adequately processed my "rape". I suffered from post-traumatic stress disorder (PTSD).

This painting portrays my parents violently, forcefully, cutting off my hair when I was 14. They held me down and shaved my head completely bald, against my protests. They raped my sense of identity and stole my innocence. They literally and figuratively amputated my connections with my teenage peers.

The colors and forms are symbolic. My body is depicted by my favorite color purple. My mother Judy, depicted by her favorite color orange, is lying on top of me; her body and her tentacle like arms are forcing me down on the ground, restraining me, entrapping me. Judy was a conspirator and accomplice to my rape. My bald shaven black head is painfully disconnected from my body, suspended in space and time. My mind and body are numb, stunned by the violent assault. I am overwhelmed by my simultaneous feelings of sadness, helplessness, impotence, fear, loathing, anger, and contempt which were invoked by this violation.

I am alone, isolated, and helpless; sucked into the vortex of a tornado, against my will. The central red tornado represents my father Edwin's dominating power, fury, vengeance, viciousness, and destruction as he orchestrated and enacted my rape.

The green hatchet protruding externally from my skull is partially buried within my head. The symbols depicting my words are indecipherable. The hatchet concretely symbolizes my baldness as my personal "Scarlet letter";

my baldness was a visible external symbol to the world of my stolen identity, my suffering, torture, confusion, struggle, disconnection, helplessness, victimization, defectiveness, unlovability, isolation, anger, and heartache.

The rape neutered me physically, socially, and emotionally. It amplified my teenage distress, anxiety, and confusion. It pushed me into the abyss; I felt lost, helpless, and hopeless, and was unable to recover my footing.

Legend for Figure 15

I painted this canvas while wearing a blindfold as a tribute to my father Edwin, for my own catharsis. My wounded heart is central in the painting; it is painfully impaled by a corkscrew and pierced by a lightning bolt. There is a large blood stain on the left emanating from my heart. The eye represents my father's literal and figurative blindness. It represents his inability to see the impact that his emotional and physical abuse had on my heart, my feelings, and my psyche. The dark and gold backgrounds represent my simultaneous existence within diametrically opposed universes; my yin and yang life realties as an adolescent; like my father's Dr. Jekyll and Mr. Hyde behavior, his rationality and irrationality; his normalcy and pathology; his lovingness and rage.

(Figure 15) You're So Blind You Can't See Zeus's Lightning Bolt

(Figure 16) The Lock Box. Emotional Abandonment

This painting used black and gold background colors. It represents a map of my psyche; it contains sharply demarcated, well contained, conscious (gold area) and unconscious worlds (black area). It also represents my external appearance to other people, and the self which I keep hidden from view.

The golden half of the picture represents my consciousness and the external image I project to the world. The square yellow area with the rainbow represents my neatly packaged conscious perfectionism and my ego. This part of my world is beautiful, luminous, bright, and colorful. The bright vivid colors represent my success, triumphs, talents, achievements, and service to others. Everything in this part of my life looks extraordinary and wonderful from the outside or at the conscious level. There is beauty, competence, stability, excellence, security, satisfaction, and happiness which is present and is visible externally to the surrounding world.

The black half of the painting represents the coexisting dark gloomy universe within my subconscious. It is not illuminated, is kept beneath the shiny surface, and is hidden from the view of my consciousness and from other people. This is a dismal part of my psychic world where anxiety, fear, shame, and anger reside. It is repressed and inaccessible.

The square blue area is deep beneath the surface, within the darkest and deepest recesses of my mind. It represents my basement or lock box, where I stuff and hide my sensitive feelings and thoughts in the repressed area of my subconscious. The Blue box with the X represents my danger zone, where I lock up and store my demons, my ultrasensitive issues and wounds. It is a "no man's land" where my unacceptable feelings are imprisoned in my maximum security "penitentiary". The shaded blue stripes and background colors represent different depths of the prominent feelings of sadness. The red represents anger, pain, and frustration. The lock represents the secure barrier to restrain these demons, so they are unable to escape. The key in the lock represents hope and a viable, visible mechanism to release the pent up, untamed, threatening, wild monsters from their lair.

(Figure 17) Geometric Stages of Grief

This painting depicts the emotional processes associated with the universal human experiences of grieving for the loss of loved ones. The four rectangular shapes represent the discrete phases of shock and denial, anger, sadness, acceptance, and bargaining. Each rectangular phase has its own predominant colors which are reflective of the emotions and experiences which dominate each stage.

The shapes and forms, however, are not all discrete or fully appreciated at first glance. There are triangular or pyramidal shapes, upright and inverted, which represent simultaneously experiencing different emotions, such as denial and anger; anger and sadness; sadness, and acceptance.

There is a central path which winds through the course of grieving. A path that is followed in the processing of the experience. The lightning bolt represents prominent sharp stabbing emotional pain and anguish. There are different shades of the blue colors; each shade represents a different depth and intensity of sadness.

The eclipse of the sun and the moon represent denial, but also symbolizes other things. The sun and the moon symbolize heavenly, divine, &/or natural processes; things we have no control over. The eclipse also represents grief triggering innate unconscious processes in which loss generates reactions and feelings that we are unable to control. Grief is an automated inherited neurological process that all humans experience. It is hard-wired into our brains.

The permanency of this image reminds us that we never completely stop grieving for our loved ones who have passed. We never stop missing them. The intensity of grief and the feelings may diminish with time; however, they never completely disappear.

Each subsequent loss cumulatively resurrects these feelings and processes.

(Figure 18) Walking Barefoot in Their Shoes

This painting depicts the concept that all humans share the same spiritual essence and are capable of deep interconnections with each other and with the spiritual universe. We are all made of the same physical substance, have the capacity for profound emotionality and spirituality, and are sensitive, imperfect, vulnerable beings. We are all naked and equal before God.

(Figure 19) Keeping an Eye Out 4 U

Eyes are recurrent important symbols in my artwork. They can represent the preciousness of sight, the emotional pain of developing blindness, denial, the inability to see or recognize certain issues; the gifts of insight, knowledge, compassion and understanding. It also symbolizes "God's Eye" a comforting loving perspective from a higher power.

(Figure 20) Leap of Faith

(Figure 21) Cardiac Bypass

This painting represents the universal human experience of suffering with emotional pain and heartbreak. We all sustain loss of loved ones, experience grief, sadness, and pain which creates emptiness inside us and a longing to reconnect.

We are each individually responsible for healing our own heartbreak, for our own emotional healing. We are each capable of acquiring the tools and skills to mend our own wounded hearts.

CHAPTER 6

Whenen I was 16 years old, and a junior in high school, Edwin waved the white flag, finally surrendering to his blindness. He sold his dental practice and entered the Center for Independent living, a transitional rehabilitation program for the blind in Manhattan. He was 47 years old.

During my entire life, Edwin had never been away from our home without Judy or another family member. Now, he was gone for 3 months of intensive retraining to adapt to his blindness and develop the skills necessary to be autonomous. It was very strange. Our family rallied to support him even though we were sad to learn that we couldn't visit him during the first 6 weeks of his residential rehabilitation stay. We spoke to him, on the phone, several times each week and enthusiastically told him how proud we were of his courage, commitment, and determination.

Edwin immersed himself in the program. He learned to read braille, type, do laundry, navigate the streets of New York with a cane, and a myriad of other skills necessary for independent living. For his final exam before graduating from the program, he was assigned a complex route to navigate in New York City but was shadowed by an instructor at a distance. The route required taking a bus, a taxi, the subway, and walking through Central Park. Given our family history, it's not surprising that we agonized over the prospect of Edwin getting mugged, injured, or lost.

We were overjoyed and relieved when he passed the test with flying colors. We were even more overjoyed when Edwin's intensive individual and group psychotherapy not only helped him adjust to his dark world, but also helped heal much of the emotional pain from his childhood, and years of emotional abuse toward his family.

Edwin was so inspired by his psychotherapy during rehabilitation that it motivated him to return to college to pursue a post-graduate degree in counseling. He wanted to work as a therapist helping other blind people. It was a new mission and a whole new career path for his life, and one none of us ever thought would happen.

We thought we had, as a family, turned the corner on the trauma and pain that had, for so long, held us in its grip. It was a small step on a road of detours and roadblocks on the journey to healing.

***

JULY 1976. PHOENIX, ARIZONA

A fresh start. That's what our move to Phoenix, Arizona represented. Against every odd that a bookmaker might make, we had been given a second chance, a new life that was ripe with the hope of great possibilities and new opportunities. What we didn't realize, at the time, was that old trauma is deeply rooted and the years of abuse we all endured would have far-reaching impact, in different ways, on our each of our lives

As a result of his therapy and regaining his independence after rehab, Edwin's rage and abuse abated; it became a thing of the past. His and Judy's relationship blossomed after the move, and the family became more cohesive than we had ever known we could be. For my part, I rationalized that the abuse I suffered was an unfortunate part of my past that couldn't be rewritten. Because Edwin was now more like the kinder, gentler father that 5-year-old Curtis remembered, I shoved the painful, ugly trauma memories into the lock box where I ignored them. *(Figure 16)*

I wiped the dust off my hands and moved forward the best I could, thinking that my issues were now resolved through the counseling I had already done. For the next 20 years, there were aftershocks of the trauma that lurked in the shadows, waiting to resurface during times of stress or emotional vulnerability. I didn't realize that they would eventually rear their ugly heads to confront me, again, after I became a parent.

***

I wasn't the only one of Edwin and Judy's children to turn to substance abuse to dull the pain of trauma. Both Andy and Dana became addicted to drugs in attempts to self-medicate and cope with the pain and trauma of what we endured. Soon, their lives spiraled out of control.

My younger sister, Dana, got involved in the druggie clique in high school and regularly abused anything she could get her hands on: Alcohol. Pot. Quaaludes, amphetamines, LSD, cocaine, and a host of other substances. It didn't take long for the drugs and alcohol to push Dana into rapid deterioration. My sweet, loving sister became irrational, combative, abusive, and irresponsible. She was 16 years old.

Ignoring my parents' pleas for her to get help for the addictions, Dana ran away from home. Out of desperation, Edwin and Judy found Dana and physically restrained her with ropes. They brought her to The Meadows in Wickenburg, Arizona, a residential addiction center. The program got through to her and Dana got sober, a commitment she would resolutely maintain for the next 25 years. The 12-Step program became the center of her universe, and the foundation of her emotional and spiritual support.

A year after Dana's recovery, my brother Andy also entered residential treatment for his own drug abuse. Andy was addicted to cocaine. His obsession with snorting coke led to his life completely unraveling. He flunked out of college, lost his job, and the experience left him standing on the edge of the same emotional cliff where I had once stood, and he decided whether to jump into the abyss or walk toward the light of healing his trauma wounds. Fortunately, Andy also committed to his journey in rehab and, like Dana, maintained his sobriety through Narcotics Anonymous for the next 25 years.

As a result of our shared trauma, each of us lived with PTSD; each of us used primitive emotional coping skills (self-medicating, running away, bullying each other) to deal with the trauma. We had isolation and distrust of others in common, as well. Separately, we each reached similar catastrophic states where we stood on the edge of the emotional cliffs screaming for help. For Mom and me, our suicide attempts were our cardinal events. For Andy and Dana, it was their drug abuse. For Edwin, it was the trauma of his childhood and his blindness.

Therapy and sobriety put us all on the road to recovery and family cohesiveness, but the deep emotional wounds and painful scars we each harbored would haunt us from the shadows and resurface in the distant future. *(Figure 11)*

CHAPTER 7

1977. TEMPE, ARIZONA

I f someone had told me, when I was a teenager, that I would attend college with my father, I'd have asked what they were smoking. Yet, here we were, Edwin and me, strolling the campus at Arizona State University as fellow students. Our shared family trauma and recovery through therapy instilled in each of us a profound desire to help others heal as we continued to heal. Edwin enrolled in a master's degree program studying counseling; since losing his vision, he wanted to counsel others who had also gone blind. I considered pursuing psychiatry but wasn't sure it was the path for me.

One thing was certain, my dad and I found a new path, together, on the ASU campus and, for the first time since I was small, our relationship blossomed. I'd guide him around campus, Edwin lovingly holding my elbow, and we talked about everything. We bonded deeply as father and son, as friends, and as peers, in a magical way that we had never experienced. It was a stark contrast—the opposite, really—of our tormented relationship of the previous 8 years. I had worshipped Edwin when I was a child, hated him during my adolescence, and despised the monstrous abuse he dragged our family through. Still, he was my father and in the complex ways that parents and children often relate, I loved him in equal measure and had empathy for how much he lost when blindness took him.

The person I walked with on the college campus was a changed man; it felt like I was finally getting to know the real Edwin beneath the decades of generational pain, abuse, and violence. We listen to music together and talked about our hopes and dreams for our lives. We became friends and I saw in Edwin the father I always thought...hoped...was underneath the abuse. It was a profound, intense new relationship for both of us.

I majored in psychology for my undergraduate degree because I wanted to explore whether psychiatry would be a good career for me. I got a job working as an orderly at a psychiatric hospital during this time. I figured it would be a good way to test the waters and I also thought that if I didn't get into medical school, I would consider a career as a clinical psychologist.

My job on the psych ward involved assisting the nurses and patients with everyday routines: bathing, serving meals, escorting patients to therapy sessions or meetings with their doctors. It was an eye-opening experience. What I saw was a never-ending cycle of prescribing medication for psychiatric diseases that only put a band-aid on the problem; it seemed they never fixed the underlying neurochemical imbalances. I'm a "fix it" kind of guy. I like clear-cut, tangible solutions to problems that can cure conditions. I quit my job at the psychiatric facility after two years and began working as an orderly in a hospital's orthopedic surgery ward.

JULY 1981

On my first day of medical school, I had an epiphany: Fear is a powerful motivator. And I was terrified. There was a massive amount of information students were required to memorize and I was terrified I wasn't up to the task, terrified that I might flunk out and my dream of becoming a doctor would disappear in a puff of smoke. No time was wasted in throwing students into the deep end of the pool by sending us into a cold anatomy lab filled with cadavers on metal tables and the acrid smell of formaldehyde in the air.

I was spellbound the first time I held a human brain in my hands. I was amazed by this homogenous, pinkish-gray, custard-like three-pound organ. This organ in my hands was the master computer of life and the seat of human consciousness that Descartes depicted as the Seat of the Soul. I wanted to discover and understand how the brain gets damaged. How it goes awry to create mental illness, dysfunctional behavior, and crippling pain. I saw the malfunctioning brain as "The Enemy", and it was one that I decided to conquer by learning everything I could about how it functions. *(Figure 12)*

I studied psychology in college with the desire to better understand myself, my family, mental illness, and to find a future career. Studying neurosciences elevated my quest to the next level. I developed an insatiable drive for knowledge regarding brain function, neuropathology, and the treatment of neurological disorders.

In medical school, I did laboratory research with David Blask, MD PhD, doing brain microsurgery during the summer break between freshman and sophomore years. The results of which were published in the journal *Experimental Neurology*. My focus, drive, and dedication to studying the brain led to an unwavering commitment to pursue a career as a neurosurgeon during my third year of medical school, eventually matched to Barrow Neurological Institute at St. Joseph's Hospital in Phoenix, Arizona. It was the best neurosurgery residency program in the country.

It would also mean that I would be back home near family, who I now had a good relationship with. It would be the best of all worlds.

***

Eggs frying in a sizzling pan. In the 1970s, it wasn't just a vision of what might be served for breakfast, it was also the centerpiece of anti-drug public service announcements. The visual analogy seared itself into the minds of a generation about the dangers of drug abuse. Variations of it ran on television depicting actors cracking eggs into the hot pan and, with a "Scared Straight" kind of seriousness. "This is your brain on drugs," the actor would say. "Any questions?"

As teenagers, my siblings and I did our fair share of drugs to escape our intolerable reality and the emotional pain we carried. The emotional and physical abuse I endured as a teenager created such anguish and, even if I wanted to address the pain—which I didn't at the time—I was ill-equipped to handle it. To survive, I locked myself in the basement—emotionally and physically. I put everything into my subconscious lock box and threw away the key.

Carrying a "Lock Box" full of compartmentalized trauma into adult life seemed to work for a time. But ignoring the sad, wounded child within me was an unsustainable tactic. I had accumulated a reservoir of painful feelings, memories, and perceptions that I never learned how to deal with in a healthy and productive manner. *(Figure 10)*

Throughout college, and most of medical school, I would often reward myself for intense studying by winding up the day with just a hit or two of weed from my bong. It allowed me to mellow and relax enough to go to bed and fall asleep quickly. I occasionally used other recreational drugs, but marijuana was my drug of choice. It was effective in small quantities, affordable, and readily accessible. It also didn't cause severe withdrawal if I stopped using abruptly; I thought it was a great choice.

I got comfortable with my habit. I deluded myself by thinking I was immune or exempt from problems of recreational drug use. I was dead wrong. This magical thinking set me up for a catastrophe that almost ruined my life and nearly destroyed my career in medicine.

In my fourth year of medical school, I traveled the country interviewing at nine prospective neurosurgery residency programs for the rigorous 7 years of subspecialty neurosurgeon training. I always brought a small baggie of weed with me to relax me and relieve the boredom. I kept my stash in my overnight bag, and wrongly assumed it was undetectable.

After interviewing at the University of North Carolina-Chapel Hill, I traveled home through the Raleigh-Durham airport, and nonchalantly placed my drug containing carry-on bag on the scanner conveyor belt, as I had done many times before. I never gave this reckless action a second thought. Part of the problem was my perception that the authorities in Raleigh were nitwits like bumbling Barney Fife (the hapless deputy to TV sheriff Andy Griffith), and that I could walk right onto the plane with the drugs in my bag.

Nope. The airport security guard scanning my bag stared intently at the screen, then asked me to step out of the line. He called to two nearby policemen. I panicked, but tried to appear calm and hoped, somehow, that I could pull off a miraculous escape.

My hopes of talking my way out of the situation were fried—like the egg in that pan—when the police discovered my drug stash, handcuffed me, read me my Miranda rights, and put me in the backseat of their patrol car. My dreams of being a neurosurgeon vaporized in a flash of marijuana smoke right before my eyes. I thought my life was over.

I was permitted one phone call before being locked up in the holding cell. I called my mother and father at home in Arizona and was both relieved and terrified when they immediately answered.

"Hello," my father said into the phone.

"Dad," I swallowed hard, "I have a problem. I'm, uh...I'm in jail in North Carolina."

"You're what?" Dad replied, incredulity in his voice.

"I did something stupid. I had a small amount of pot in my bag, and they caught it on the airport scanners."

"Oh, my God. Judy," he called to my mother. "It's Curtis, he's in trouble." Dad turned back to the phone. "Ok, here's what we're going to do: we're going to fly to Raleigh on the next available flight and get the bail money. We'll get you out of there."

I was relieved that they rallied to my side without blinking an eye. My parents were coming to rescue me. Within an hour, a guard informed me that a bail bondsman was on his way. It took two hours for him to arrive, but it felt like two hundred. He told me that my parents were already on a plane and had hired a top-notch local defense attorney to take my case. He then took me to a hotel for the night.

I lay in bed, in the hotel room, and stared up at the popcorn ceiling tiles as my whole world swirled around me. Every time a toilet flushed in the next room, I imagined my life and career dreams swirling down the toilet with the water. My worst fears had become a painful reality. I lay in bed and cried for hours. I'm glad I didn't have any means of committing suicide that night because I might have ended it all if I'd had the opportunity. Eventually, I fell asleep.

I was awakened by the sound of knocking on the hotel room door; my parents had arrived. Edwin and Judy saw my desperation and immediately comforted me. My father, tears in his eyes, held me as I sobbed. It was one of the few times I remember ever seeing Edwin cry. They both assured me of their love, and they would do whatever it took to help me overcome the mess I created.

This was the most defining moment of my relationship with my parents. Everything hit the proverbial fan and it had splattered all over me. I made the worst mess of my life, and my parents still loved me and were determined to help me recover and climb out of the hole I had dug. They were my saving grace, that day. My strength and my solace.

After meeting with the attorney, we returned to Arizona, and I resumed medical school. I tried to pretend that everything was normal. I told few people what had happened. When I returned to Raleigh for the court hearing six weeks later, I plead guilty to misdemeanor drug possession and was released from custody with community service and drug counseling. To put it bluntly: I got off easy compared to what could have happened.

It was a wakeup call, and I listened. I stopped using drugs entirely and replaced it with a daily exercise habit. As a natural painkiller, the endorphins were good for me. Once I found a healthier way of medicating myself, I turned into an exercise addict. I substituted endurance races and triathlons for drugs.

My work also became my addiction; I became a workaholic. Work as a neurosurgeon is a high-stakes, dramatic, high-energy job. Neurosurgery residency training is a 7 year-long marathon that requires intellectual, physical, and emotional endurance. Throughout most of my life, until middle age, I didn't recognize that I was still medicating myself daily with exercise and work. I was still avoided my lock box of trauma and had never confronted my issues or learned to manage my feelings in a healthy way. My ignorance was not bliss.

I graduated from medical school at the top of my class, and it was an exciting time of achievement and possibilities for the future. Little did I know that this epic moment in my life would be the last milestone I would celebrate with my father, Edwin.

CHAPTER 8

Neurosurgery attracts a certain personality type: the perfectionist and overachievers; the Type-A personalities who are curious, meticulous, detail-oriented, and those with OCD traits. Most neurosurgeons are strong, dominant people who value being in control. We are the "Captains of the Ship". We're comfortable making life and death decisions under extreme stress and in complicated circumstances.

My neurosurgery residency required 100% effort and commitment: a total immersion. From a subconscious standpoint, my success in neurosurgery was the ultimate validation to rebut the Zeus's injury to my ego as a child. However, I didn't understand it at the time. I just loved my career success and was determined to nurture it further. After my parents' unflinching support after the Raleigh arrest, I looked forward to sharing my successes with Edwin and Judy.

But it wasn't to be. In the second year of residency training, my first year of neurosurgery residency, the bottom began to fall out of my world again.

***

The telephone rang.

"Hello?" I said.

"Curtis?" My mother's voice was ragged and emotional. "We have to take your dad to the emergency room right away." She began to sob.

"Mom, take a breath, ok? What's going on?" I was already pulling my socks and shoes on, ready to head out the door.

"I don't know," she said, trying to catch her breath. "He's acting so bizarre. Psychotic, almost. He's agitated and incoherent. I can't handle him. Can you come."

It was a Saturday, one of my rare days off work. I was overworked, exhausted, and stressed. But there was no choice. "Of course, Mom. I'm on my way."

When I arrived, we tried to calm him, but it didn't work. So, we drove him to the emergency room at the hospital where I worked and had him admitted to the psychiatric ward. The psychiatrist diagnosed him with psychotic depression.

My mother said his delirium rose quickly. I hadn't observed the problem firsthand because I'd been focused on the residency and had spent little time visiting my parents in recent days. Edwin was so agitated and combative that the doctors locked him in a padded isolation room and tied him with four-point leather restraints. They plied him with sedatives and antidepressants which calmed the agitation but worsened his disorientation and confusion.

Next, the psychiatrist treated him with Electroconvulsive Shock Therapy (ECT); literally shocking his brain with strong electrical currents. This didn't help at all, in fact, it made his condition significantly worse. Edwin had seizures, drooled, made nonsensical comments, and exhibit inappropriate behavior like defecating and urinating in the hallway. He had no idea where he was or what was happening. He was a zombie who could not communicate with us or even feed himself.

It was horrendous.

Edwin deteriorated rapidly. He developed spontaneous grand mal seizures and fell and hit his head. We presumed that he became suddenly depressed due to his blindness and inability to get into graduate school to become a clinical psychologist. His rapid mental deterioration and seizures were red flags to me. I was determined to help him and make sense of this tragic mess.

I suspected that the psychiatrist had misdiagnosed Edwin; his condition didn't seem to present as psychotic depression, especially with the seizures as one of the symptoms. I requested an CAT scan of Edwin's brain to determine if he had sustained a subdural hematoma from his fall, or if there was some other structural brain lesion causing the seizures. The scan showed no structural lesions but did show diffuse brain shrinkage. Edwin had severe brain atrophy.

Since Edwin had previously worked as a dentist, he was exposed to all sorts of pathogens. I thought he might possibly have Jacob-Creutzfeld (JC) Disease which is a rapidly fatal encephalopathy caused by tiny virus-like structures called prion particles. These infect the brain and is similar to Mad Cow Disease. It's transmitted by direct contact to brain tissue.

It was also possible, and I thought more likely, that Edwin had Alzheimer's Disease, which was consistent with his diffuse brain atrophy shown on the CAT scan. I insisted that a brain biopsy be performed, which is the only definitive way to diagnose Alzheimer's Disease, and to differentiate it from Jacob-Creutzfeld Disease.

It was surreal to have my father scheduled for a neurosurgical procedure, a frontal craniotomy to biopsy his brain. This was my domain. I was the fledgling neurosurgeon. But I was in shock and denial. I also knew I couldn't have personal involvement in his surgery. I was too close as a family member.

Edwin went to another competent neurosurgeon I trusted. I couldn't bear to watch dad's surgery, and I didn't want my co-residents and teaching attending physicians to know of my father's turmoil. Or my own. The pain all went into the lock box.

Edwin's brain biopsy demonstrated amyloid plaques and neurofibrillary tangles, confirmation of Alzheimer's Disease. It was initially a relief that it was "only" garden variety Alzheimer's and not a rapidly fatal disease like JC. However, in retrospect, it may have been more humane and tolerable in the end. Alzheimer's is often referred to as The Long Goodbye. And it is devastating.

This seemed a cruel and painful chapter on which Edwin would end his long and troubled life. Edwin's devastating disorientation and confusion was exponentially compounded by his blindness.

We normally rely on our vision to provide extensive sensory cues which orient us to our environment. Edwin lived in darkness and now, the light bulb in his brain was slowly dimming as well. We grieved as we watched him slip away a little more every day. He lived in a nursing home for four years. He died one year before I finished my residency.

***

At the end of the four-year stay in the nursing home, we decided to provide in-home care for Edwin. Judy installed a mechanical Hoyer life in their backyard to help Edwin get in and out of the swimming pool. He always loved to swim, and we were determined to provide him with some basic joy and fun. I came over to visit my parents a few times each month, usually on weekends. I took my father swimming every chance I got.

Edwin was calm when he was in the pool, and I knew life-saving techniques, so we were comfortable swimming gently in the deeper water in the pool. It's bittersweet how life circles back around. Where I was once the small boy being taught to swim by my father, I was now the one guiding dad through the pool. The caretaker and protector. I was the one who gave the submarine rides now. Our roles were now reversed.

"Dive! Dive! Dive!" I would announce joyfully, just like Edwin would do when I was five years old. Edwin would hold my shoulders and ride above the surface of the water.

We found the same loving connection now as we had twenty-five years earlier. Our swimming soothed us. It reconnected us physically, emotionally, and spiritually. It's a time in our lives that I will treasure forever. *(Figure 1)*

CHAPTER 9

J udy called me on Sunday morning March 31st, 1991. Edwin had a high fever and was being admitted to the hospital. My wife, Celeste, and I went there immediately. When I saw my father in the hospital room, his body was present, but his mind was gone. His brain had shrunk to less than half its normal size and was no longer functioning. He was unable to communicate, walk, eat, or drink.

I held his hand and gently stroked his forehead. I wept and told him how much I loved him. Even though he didn't react or acknowledge me, I believe he heard me. That he felt my touch and my love for him.

I was working as chief neurosurgery resident on call that weekend and trying to fight off a bout with the flu. With my father in the hospital, I really wanted to stay by his side, but when duty calls, you answer. I got a call that a 27-year-old man arrived in the hospital emergency room with a strange injury: a Bic pen through his right eye into his brain. He said he chose to commit suicide through his eye because he wanted to stop his frightening visual hallucinations. He wanted to end his tortured life.

He had pounded the pen deeply into his skull using the palm of his right hand; only a half inch of the pen protruded from his eye. It was shocking to see him with the pen barely protruding from his face. His right eye was paralyzed, useless, and bloody. The pen injured the optic nerve which blinded his right eye. It had also punctured the cavernous sinus and compressed the right internal carotid artery providing blood supply to the right half of his brain. Amazingly, the pen did not penetrate through any brain tissue, cause major bleeding, a stroke, or brain damage.

My attending neurosurgeon, Joe Zabramaski, and I spent 7 hours carefully exposing and surgically extracting the pen. The operation involved removing part of the skull and bone of the eye socket to access the brain, eye, and deep nerves and blood vessels at the base of the brain. Toward the end of the surgery, my flu symptoms and fatigue became severe. I scrubbed out of the case early and went home to rest.

It was 11:30pm and I had just crawled into bed. I was almost asleep when my phone rang. Judy, distraught and weeping, told me Edwin had just died.

How ironic. On the day I tried to save the life of a psychotic man who wanted to destroy his own eye and take his life, I lost my blind father. Edwin's situation was, paradoxically, the opposite: he wanted to live. He wanted to restore his vision, overcome his emotional issues, and rebuild his life. Sadly, I was helpless to intervene in either of their circumstances. I was impotent; I could not relieve their suffering, restore their vision, sanity, health, or lives.

I immediately went to the hospital to see Edwin before he was transported to the morgue. He was finally at peace. In my work as a neurosurgeon, I often pronounced patients dead, and was comfortable with this process. However, this was profoundly different. This cold, lifeless corpse was my father.

Counseling tremendously helped me understand and healthily process the diverse feelings and thoughts associated with grief and the loss of my family. I continue to grieve for the loss of my father to this day, even though it has been 32 years since he died. I miss my father Edwin and am now comforted by my memories of him, his paintings, his life, and his love. He lives on in my heart, my mind, and this story. These are Edwin's legacies.

***

One month after Edwin died, my mother decided to give Andy, Dana, and me a few of our father's treasured things. Among them were three paintings that Edwin created in 1978 while blind. Andy got one. So did Dana. And so, did I. *(Figures 1-3)*

The painting I received is called *Heaven Over the Ocean* which has been extremely meaningful to me. In the piece, the moon and stars are reflected off the ocean as it laps at the beach. The water symbolizes my love for my father, and the memories of swimming with Edwin, submarine rides and all. I hung Edwin's painting in my bathroom where it would be a daily reminder of his love for me and a visible symbol of my ongoing connection with my dad.

Andrew inherited the painting called *West Maui Mountains*. Dana inherited the painting called *Sunset Over Monument Valley*. I didn't realize that I would inherit these paintings from Andy and Dana in the near future, after they both died under tragic circumstances due their addictions and mental illness.

***

My mother sold the house in Scottsdale shortly after Edwin died—it was too large for her to live in alone, and it was filled with memories of Edwin's tragic illness. She moved to Sun City where she bought a 2-bedroom home. Andy lived in Kansas City where he attended medical school. Dana lived in Phoenix where she worked as a masseuse and a paralegal. I continued my residency training in neurosurgery. Our lives seemed to return to normal, or as close to it after losing a parent. My siblings maintained their sobriety and their future careers and lives seemed promising.

Chinese food literally and figurative became my mother's downfall. One afternoon, Judy slipped and fell as she walked out of a Chinese restaurant. She fractured her right shoulder and was hospitalized to have her shattered right shoulder replaced.

Her diabetes and obesity predisposed her to develop a wound infection. Within a month of her surgery, she developed a severe staph infection which involved her surgical wound, the shoulder prosthesis, and the surrounding bone. The infection was called osteomyelitis. Her artificial shoulder had to be removed, and she was treated with intravenous antibiotics for 6 months to cure the bone infection. After 3 months, her orthopedist fused her right shoulder because he thought there was a very high chance that a new artificial shoulder would become reinfected.

Meanwhile, after I finished my residency training in June 1992, Celeste and I settled into our new lives, a modest 4-bedroom home, and parenthood. Our first child, Alexander Samuel Dickman, was born in May 1993. Rachel Suzanne Dickman came along a couple of years later in February 1995. Grandma Judy was enthralled over her grandchildren, and we often reminisced how Edwin would have adored them, too. I thought of Edwin every time I took my children on submarine rides in our swimming pool.

Life was clicking along the way I always imagined it would: a meaningful, successful career healing people, and a beautiful family I loved. Still, I began to suspect something was seriously wrong. I frequently felt anxious, empty, and troubled. I tried to deny the feelings that the demons in the lock box would not rest. It wasn't until Judy died that I began to confront the baggage from my trauma.

Eventually, Judy's morbid obesity and arthritis of the hips, knees, and feet, led to her inability to walk. She weighed almost 400 pounds and was unable to walk or exercise. She had a delivery service and a home health care assistant supply her with Chinese food regularly. Her overall health deteriorated due to her obesity, diabetes, hypertension, and chronic depression. She also developed several small ischemic strokes in her brain. These medical problems eventually rendered her bed ridden.

We decided to move my mother to a nursing home after multiple falls out of her bed. In fact, Judy fell out of bed four times in one week and lay helpless on the bedroom floor unable to get up. The paramedics were summoned to her home each time. Due to her weight, it took four paramedics to lift her and carry her to her bed. We finally convinced her to sell her home and move to Kivel Nursing Home.

The staff at Kivel had expertly cared for Edwin for several years, and they were the only Jewish nursing facility in our area. They served kosher food and even had their own clergy in residence, Rabbi Martin Sharf. He had performed my father's funeral service. Judy liked these features about Kivel but resisted living in a nursing home due to the belief that her mother, Bessie, had died from nursing home neglect.

Ever the foodie, Judy perpetually complained about the food at Kivel. When Celeste and I visited every Sunday, with our children, we brought Chinese food to appease and comfort her. At this stage of life, it didn't seem that Chinese food would do her any additional harm, and her comfort food was the major joy in her life along with her children and grandchildren.

Judy had a lot of chutzpah. She was banned from the communal dining room at Kivel several times because she stole food from the other residents' trays. Needless to say, this caused conflict with the other residents and the staff. Occasionally, we would find Judy sitting in the hallway, alone, outside the main dining hall, eating her dinner in solitary confinement due to her food snatching. It was both heartbreaking and hysterically funny. She lived up to her nickname, "Judy the Foodie".

Ironically, Kivel was fundraising to construct a new dining hall for the residents. In a wonderful stroke of getting two birds with one stone, Celeste and I donated the funds for construction and, when the dining hall was completed, it was named The Edwin and Judith Dickman Dining Hall and it served as a communal place for meals and Jewish holiday celebrations. Not only was it the perfect way to memorialize my father, but I also figured it would be much harder for the staff to kick my mother out of a dining room that had her name on it.

My mother lived in Kivel nursing home for the last five years of her life. She had several small strokes during her last 6 months of life, and became disinterested in food, even Chinese food. This was the cardinal sign that she didn't have much time left. On June 6, 2001, at Hospice of the Valley, Judy passed away.

Andy and Dana would die less than a decade after my mom, under identical circumstances to Judy, but with the added complications of self-destructive addictions, severe depression, and self- induced medical illnesses. *(Figure 11)* Within short order, I would become the sole survivor of my family.

✳✳✳

One month after my mother died, I competed in a Half-Ironman Triathlon at Camp Pendleton, north of San Diego, California. The water seemed slightly choppy during the morning of the race, but I didn't notice any big waves. I donned my racing wetsuit which provided buoyancy, kept me warm, and increased my swimming speed. I went out for a five-minute warm up swim before the race without incident.

I entered the ocean with a group of 50 other racers. The water was freezing, and I noticed moderate-sized wave swells ahead of me. None of the other swimmers appeared to have any difficulty with the waves, so I wasn't initially alarmed. The designated swimming course was marked by large, pyramid shaped, inflatable plastic orange buoys. The swim route was also lined by men in kayaks and small life rafts at 50-yard intervals who served as rescuers if the need arose.

Even though I warmed up earlier to accommodate to the water temperature, the ice-cold saltwater shocked me as I dove beneath its dark surface. I swam into deeper water and immediately felt "air hunger" due to my sudden burst of muscle activity and the surge of ice water around my body. I swam for a few minutes and had still not yet fully caught my breath. Without realizing it, I was entering an area where 25-foot waves broke.

Suddenly I felt the wave crash down upon me, and I was instantly submerged deep below the waterline. I was surrounded by cold blackness, and quickly became disoriented. I was trapped and had no idea which way was up. My life flashed before my eyes and I sent up a desperate prayer: "God, please don't let me die. I have so much more I want to do with my life."

Instinctively, I arched my back, stretched out my body, and held both arms straight above my head as I prayed for a miracle to keep me alive. I waited and prayed, suspended beneath the cold water for what seemed like an eternity. As my hope of surviving began to dwindle, my head suddenly emerged above the surface of the water, and I gratefully gasped the precious fresh air.

I looked for a rescue boat but was unable to see one over the swells. I swam out further toward deeper water to find a lifeboat, and found myself in relatively calm water, beyond the breaking waves. I found a yellow rescue kayak where I rested for a few minutes while I regained my composure and let my adrenaline surge and fear subside. I collected my thoughts and my emotions during my few minutes of rest.

I was inspired to resume the race and to resume my life; to never give up hope. I resumed swimming and finished the triathlon. I was relieved when my feet hit the warm grainy sand on the beach, and I was happy to be back on dry land again. I was grateful that God had answered my prayers and had given me a reprieve.

The near drowning would become a metaphor for the inner turmoil bubbling up from my lock box of trauma. On the surface of my life, everything looked perfect. I had enormous success in my medical career, wealth, and a beautiful wife and children. I seemingly had it all, yet emotionally, I was drowning in PTSD. *(Figure 13)*

During the previous years, my emotional problems continued to mount; they had become a cumulative pile of trauma. I was submerged in my anxiety and distress, and barely came up for the occasional gasp of emotional air before I was submerged again by the next crisis or problem. My life was swirling out of control. My mother's recent death had compounded my unresolved feelings of grief for my father. It stirred my subconscious and caused my lock box of emotions to burst wide open.

CHAPTER 10

M y anxiety and depression were complicated by emotional burnout. The crises just seemed to keep hitting, after the death of my parents, I settled a malpractice suit out of court because I didn't have the emotional strength to fight it even though I could defend my actions. I was sucked into an emotional tornado which was spinning around violently inside my mind, wreaking havoc.

I felt trapped by my ineffectiveness to deal with the progressive crises and desperately wanted to escape. I began to fantasize about committing suicide to escape my pain, but never seriously considered acting out the fantasy.

I considered leaving medicine completely and finding a new career. I wanted to run away and have less stress in my life. I thought a new job was the answer. I was confused and suffering. I had reached the end of my emotional rope and didn't know where to turn. I didn't realize that a new career was not the answer. I couldn't run away from the demons in my lock box. I needed professional help. I scheduled an urgent appointment with a psychiatrist.

The first appointment was 13 years and 2 days after my father, Edwin, died. I don't think it was a coincidence that my failure to adequately grieve for Edwin, or to process the trauma of my past, played a substantial role in my emotional crises. My therapist, Dr. K, frequently asked me the poignant question: "Why now?"

We started with what seemed to be the primary issues: The deaths of my parents, the stress of the malpractice suits, work stresses, inadequate parenting skills, severe anxiety, and burnout. I desperately wanted to escape my life. I was overwhelmed by my feelings and circumstances. Occasionally, we zoomed out and took a bird's eye overview of the major life events, milestones, and trauma. At Dr. K's request, I diagrammed the timeline of my life which included all the important life events from an emotional standpoint. This included all my life's traumas and the good and bad circumstances of my life.

The diagram served as our roadmap for future discussions and allowed Dr. K to guide and steer my therapy with an adequate view of the overall perspective. It also allowed me to connect the dots and reframe the relevance and impact of my past experiences, perceptions, and feelings in a healthier, holistic perspective. I began to re-experience and analyze the painful life journey, and slowly process my life traumas. It started me on the road to healing these deep emotional wounds.

As an adult, I never consciously recognized or thought about most of the life traumas I have endured. I had repressed and denied many of the experiences during most of my life. I banished these painful memories to the lock box because they were too distressing to think about. The primary tools we used to tap into my subconscious were dream analysis and therapeutic painting. Both processes were fascinating and productive. These processes opened a virtual window for us to peer into the inner recesses of my mind.

Prior to beginning therapy, I didn't fully appreciate the value of dreaming and dream analysis. I rarely remembered any of my prior dreams and never, ever wrote down the content of my dreams. I had a few recurring dream themes throughout my life.

As a boy, I had recurring vivid dreams of ugly, frightening monsters that chased me and tried to hurt me. I was anxious and panicked as I ran, trying to escape these threats. After I started therapy, I was able to put these dreams in context and understand their meaning. These dreams resulted from my "Zeus injury", my early suffering from rejection from my father. The monsters represented my fears of inadequacy, unlovability, defectiveness, unworthiness, persecution, torture, and harm.

When I was in high school, I had recurring vivid dreams of myself wearing a white coat; I fought with my own "clone", as we grappled to maintain possession of a reel-to-reel tape recorder. These dreams represented my conscious struggle to decide whether to pursue a career as a musician or a doctor. They represented my inner conflict and struggles regarding my identity and my career path. I was trying to define who I was.

My most poignant recurring dream began after I graduated from my neurosurgery residency and began practicing neurosurgery. I dreamt of being trapped in a school, wandering the halls aimlessly, feeling helpless, frustrated, and anxious, as I tried to figure out what classes I needed to take to graduate. I initially ignored this highly symbolic dream for a long time before I understood its meaning. My subconscious was telling me that I needed to heal my emotional wounds, to learn about my personal issues, and to discard my own "emotional baggage". It was important that I clearly recognized that my education was incomplete; something was crucially missing.

After I made a commitment to pursue intensive therapy, Dr. K instructed me to pay attention to my dreams, and to record dream content in detail, so we could analyze and discuss them during therapy. She indicated my dreams would provide very important psychodynamic clues about my subconscious thoughts and feelings; they would guide my therapy and facilitate my progress.

I quickly became adept at remembering my dreams. Once I got "dialed in to my dream channel", it provided the most amazing corridor to my subconscious, and supercharged my progress during therapy.

The more I developed this skill, the easier it became. Initially, I was satisfied if I could vividly remember 1 or 2 dreams each week. Within a few months, I was able to remember 1 or 2 dreams per night. At the height of my therapy, I was able to remember up to 7 dreams per night in exquisite detail.

I applied my perfectionism, obsessive compulsive traits, and overachieving mentality to my therapy and my dream analysis; just like I did to everything else in my life. These are the attitudes that made me successful in medical school, residency, and my career. After all, what patient would ever want to their neurosurgeon to have anything less than perfect technical skills, intellectual knowledge, and judgment? I wouldn't let anyone operate on my brain unless they were a perfectionist.

One of the biggest gifts I derived from therapy was learning to acknowledge, accept, and forgive myself for my imperfections and my mistakes. Although this sounds logical and easy to do; it was a very difficult thing for me to do. Turns out, it is actually very hard to teach a perfectionist that it's OK to be imperfect.

***

I began painting in 2001, 10 years after my father passed away. Although I wasn't consciously aware of the association at the time, it wasn't a coincidence that I began painting on the anniversary of his death. I started on a whim, out of curiosity, but my painting endeavors were inspired by Edwin's beautiful paintings.

I vividly remember the day I saw my father's paintings for the first time at Edwin's first art show at Arizona State University. Even though he was blind, he created paintings with astounding clarity, beauty, and detail. *(Figures 1-3)* On this day in 2001, I had wondered out loud to my wife, Celeste, "If dad could paint blind, what kind of paintings could I create with being able to see?

Next thing I knew, I was painting daily, an intense passion and drive propelling me forward, I woke at four o'clock in the morning and painted for several hours before going to the hospital to spend long days in surgery. I created approximately 20 acrylic paintings within a short time span, and I was hooked.

When I started psychotherapy, Dr. K was greatly impressed that I painted and had been inspired to do so by my father who had painted without his vision. Dr. K immediately seized this opportunity to utilize art as a modality for therapy; she asked me to use my painting as a tool to augment my therapy. By the second therapy session, she requested samples of my painting. Then, she began giving me art assignments relevant to the issues I wrestled with in therapy.

My first assignment was to grab the bull by the horns, so to speak, and confront my OCD and perfectionism.

"I want you to paint from your heart," she said. "Use large brushes and palate knives. Focus on using broad, bold, strokes. Just let the piece take shape organically. Don't plan it. Don't sketch it out first or obsess over perfection. Let your emotions drive what you put on the canvas."

***

When I got home, I turned on Led Zeppelin (Stairway to Heaven and Rock and Roll) and began painting. Classic Rock music was my favorite release, and it reminded me of playing guitar when I was a teenager. I let go of the precise techniques I used in my other paintings and just went with the flow of the music. It was an emotional catharsis I hadn't expected. I was amazed at the raw power and beauty of what was pouring out of me. The piece that resulted from this assignment, *Rape of Adolescent Innocence,* was a significantly emotional piece for me. *(Figure 14)*

The painting is an abstract of my parents holding me down and cutting all my hair off when I was a teenager. They shaved my head bald. The colors and forms are a symbolic collage of abstract shapes. My body is depicted in my favorite color, purple. My mother, Judy, represented in her favorite color, orange, lay on top of me, her body and arms are tentacle-like, forcing me down onto the ground. Restraining me. Judy was a conspirator and accomplice to my assault.

My shaven head is black and amputated from my body, suspended in space and time. My mind and body are numb, stunned by the violence. I am overwhelmed by simultaneous feelings of impotence, fear, and loathing.

The painting provided a tremendous amount of insight and allowed for important personal advances in my therapy. It was the first experience of opening the lock box and letting my demons loose from my subconscious. There was a healing freedom in the act of creating this painting, and it was a revelation.

Around my disconnected body, there's a swirling tornado of red, the dominating power, viciousness and destruction tearing my identity from me: my father, Edwin.

A green hatchet is embedded in my skull, symbolic as the instrument of my personal "Scarlet Letter branding"; my baldness, a visible external symbol to the world of my stolen identity and the torture I suffered. The symbols depicting my words are indecipherable.

While I had enjoyed painting for years, using my art as a therapeutic tool was a catharsis for emotional healing I had not expected. This assignment helped me process my parents' vicious assault that had amplified my teenage distress and anxiety and left me feeling helpless and hopeless. It also helped me recognize, and begin to address, the perfectionistic and obsessive traits that had driven me for so long.

The painting gave Dr. K and me an immense amount of insight and was a catalyst for important personal advances in my therapy as I liberated repressed painful memories by opening the lock box that held my demons.

It was only the beginning.

***

My second assignment was to paint blindfolded; to walk a mile in my father's shoes, so to speak. The goal was to release my repressed and complicated feelings regarding my relationship with my father. This was a difficult and challenging assignment for me. I wanted to be in control, and I had a hard time relinquishing that control to create this painting. Instead of just letting go, I compromised. *(Figure 15)*

Before starting the painting blindfolded, I painted the left half of the canvas black, and the right half gold. I used masking tape to create a precise, sharply demarcated edge between the two colors. I chose vivid colors for different meanings: Red for the blood, heartbreak, turmoil, and pain; yellow for the blindness, tears, and lightning; purple—my favorite color—represented my suffering, suppression, and denial of my childhood trauma and abuse.

Celeste helped me put the blindfold on and handed the different paint colors to me as I requested them. She also oriented me to the canvas. I didn't use a paintbrush with this painting, instead, I finger-painted like a 5-year-old would do. It helped me connect to the 5-year-old boy inside me that was tragically wounded by my father's rejection, causing Zeus's lightning bolt to pierce my heart.

The images of this painting had important symbolism—a wounded heart impaled by a corkscrew and a lightning bolt; a large blood stain; and an eye representing my father's literal and figurative blindness and his inability to see the impact his emotional and physical abuse had on me. The black and gold background represented my existence in diametrically opposed universes, my yin and yang life realities as an adolescent and my father's Jekyll and Hyde behavior.

My third assigned painting was a surprise. We were discussing my childhood fear of abandonment and my hypersensitivity to perceived rejection, and how they persisted into my adult life.

"Go home and paint your abandonment," Dr. K. Said, somewhat cryptically.

"What exactly do you mean?"

"Paint what you know and feel about your abandonment," she replied, again, very cryptic.

"I'm not sure what you want. I need a little more detail than that."

"You know what your issues are. Figure out what you want to paint, and then go home, blast some music like before, and paint it."

"Blast music, like before, and paint," I repeated, nodding. She noted my frown and smiled gently.

I left Dr. K's office unsure whether I could just let go the way she wanted me to. At home, I contemplated the situation. I knew from the first two assignments that my hypersensitivity to perceived abandonment and rejection were based on the early childhood wounds. Those that created the deeply held subconscious beliefs that I was defective, inadequate, unlovable, and completely unworthy of love at all. The denial of my trauma, and its impact on me, were key contributors to the dysfunction and dissatisfaction in my current life. But I had no clue how to connect the dots of these problems and resolve them, even though I had gained insight into what the issues were.

The painting that emerged from this assignment is a stark, sharply geometric piece titled *The Lock Box. Emotional Abandonment.* *(Figure 16)* I used the same black and gold background colors as in my blindfolded painting. I envisioned this piece as a map of my psyche delineating the conscious, well-contained areas of myself (the gold area) and my deep, long-neglected unconscious world (the black area).

The gold half of the picture is the external image I project to the world. It is neatly packaged with conscious perfectionism and my ego. This part of my world is luminous and colorful; the vivid rainbow colors represent my triumphs, talents, and service to others. Everything about it looks wonderful from the outside, conscious level. There is beauty, stability, excellence, and satisfaction.

The black half of the painting is the coexisting dark and gloomy universe within my subconscious. It is a repressed, inaccessible region until one reaches the blue square area, deep beneath the surface. This is my lock box, the place where the darkest, most sensitive feeling and trauma are submerged in my subconscious. The X—comprised of red to symbolize anger and pain and blue to represent differing depths of sadness—is the danger zone where my demons are locked. The key in the lock is hope, a viable and visible mechanism to release the wild, threatening monsters from their lair.

***

The fourth painting assignment came out of left field. Where the previous assignments had focused on trauma related to my birth family, this assignment would encompass grief over the impending loss of my therapist, Dr. K. She had prepared me for weeks in advance of the event, but she was ill and her condition—a crippling cardiac condition—made it impossible to continue working. It was necessary for her to retire.

My first reactions to the news were strong; I was stunned. Panicked, really. And Sad and anxious. All these feelings hit me at once. Then, my mind switched to denial.

"This can't be true. It's not happening," I said. I rapidly transitioned to resentment and anger. I would be abandoned. Again. By someone I trusted with my heart and my most sensitive secrets. I cycled through all these emotions several times. It felt like emotional whiplash.

"I'm sad, too, Curtis," she said, tears in her eyes. "But I have no choice." And she gently guided me through the process of identifying my thoughts and feelings, modeling the appropriate way process them in a healthy manner, and move toward acceptance.

During the first of our final sessions, after she disclosed her imminent retirement, she asked me to paint my grief. I didn't want to. I was mad at her and didn't want to accept that she was about to abandon me, leaving me stranded. But I trusted Dr. K, and I knew painting would help me now, as it had throughout our therapeutic relationship.

I went home that evening and thought about everything I experienced after Dr. K dropped the bomb on me. The aftershocks of the emotions shook me to the core, and I was in no mood to keep thinking about these profound, intense feelings. So, I slept on it, hoping that, with the sunrise, I would feel more rested and able to process the emotions.

When I awoke the next morning, I developed a vision and plan for this assignment. I decided to base the work on Dr. Elisabeth Kubler-Ross's stages of grief described in her book "On Death and Dying": Denial, anger, bargaining, depression, and acceptance. As a neurosurgeon, I understood these processes from an intellectual perspective. But I was still naive about appropriate grieving.

I had sustained many losses in my life, but my role models never taught me how to process grief in a healthy way. My family denied and suppressed their feelings, or they lashed out in an emotional flood of abuse. I had a lot to learn.

For this painting, I returned to my carefully designed and meticulously planned creative process; the habitually perfectionistic painter re-emerged. The result is a piece titled *Geometric Stages of Grief. (Figure 17)*

The geometric shapes and overlapping patterns of colors represented the distinct stages of grief, and the simultaneous presence of my feelings and pain. There were several symbols I used to represent this journey through grief: a central meandering path in a thunderbolt pattern represented my pain and my anger. An eclipse and a rainbow represented denial and acceptance. I painted two identical canvases; I kept one for myself and gave the other to Dr. K. It was a fitting tribute and gift of gratitude to her for our therapeutic journey together, for which I will always be grateful.

It turns out that this painting would become a tool to help me process future grief; I would need these new coping skills sooner than I anticipated. In the not-too-distant future, I would need to navigate the losses of my brother and sister after they each committed suicide.

***

Dr. K helped me transition to a new clinical psychologist she recommended, Dr. Linda Hirsch, PhD. It turns out that she was the perfect therapist to guide me through my enduring journey of emotional healing. When I transitioned my therapy to Linda, I was apprehensive about sharing with her. Building trust is an important part of the therapeutic relationship and, after years with Dr. K—whose loss I was still grieving—I was now back at Square One in the trust-building process with a new therapist.

It took time, and my therapy progressed slowly—sometimes, my anger and resentment toward Linda for not being Dr K.—and my guilt for having these irrational thoughts and feelings—kept me from taking her good advice onboard. I often didn't listen to what she said, and I proverbially shot myself in the foot on more than one occasion.

It took months to develop absolute trust in Linda, but once it happened, my progress blossomed like a flower. Although, the flower still had its share of painful thorns. Thinking back, it was more like a Jumping Cholla Cactus that latched onto my bare skin and refused to relinquish its piercing hold on me.

Ultimately, I spent seven more years working with Linda, vigorously working through intense sessions—sometimes double sessions that each lasted an hour and forty-five minutes rather than the customary 50 minutes. It is an ongoing journey; thus I will always need to confront my triggers and sensitivities related to my abuse trauma. They are part of me, yet do not define who I am.

I have spent my adult life focusing on an absolute commitment to heal others, to ameliorate pain and suffering, to cure disease, and to compassionately reach out and touch the hearts and souls of my patients. My intentions and actions have been genuine and pure. My life is devoted to Tikkun Olam; healing and mending the world.

Emotional healing is a work in progress. There is one painting of mine that depicts the concept that all humans share the same spiritual essence and are capable of deep interconnections with each other and with the spiritual universe. It's called *Walking Barefoot in Their Shoes*. *(Figure 18)*

There are four human legs in vivid colors: red, green, blue, and purple. The different color legs symbolize the variety of interpersonal and intercultural differences throughout the world. Every human leg and foot have the same basic form and shape, depicting our common physical, emotional, and spiritual human essence. The feet touch each other, symbolizing the community of our global village of humanity. We are all made of the same stuff, and we are sensitive, imperfect, vulnerable beings. We are all naked and equal before God.

The contours of the limbs fit together, and are intertwined in an intimate, complementary, and symbiotic way. This symbolizes our individual responsibilities and communal capacity to reach out and help, to heal each other's spiritual and emotional wounds. Through our cooperation, compassion, and interconnection, we can solve the world's greatest problems and achieve Tikkun Olam. We can heal, repair, and transform our world.

***

EPILOGUE

"How did you ever forgive your father, and move past the pain he inflicted on you and your family?" A friend asked me. This is a poignant question with a complex answer.

In this story, I bare my soul and my psyche. There is tremendous value in going out on an emotional limb. I didn't think anyone goes through life unscathed; most people hold onto their stories, deep inside, and never confront, process, or share their issues. I think most parents have learned unhealthy parenting methods from their own parents and, when you don't know better, you unconsciously pass what you've learned down to the generations that come after you.

I forgave Edwin, and Judy, for the pain they inflicted on me because I truly believe they genuinely loved me with all their hearts. They did the best they were capable of. They had tremendous emotional baggage of their own—their own tsuris, which is Yiddish for woes—and I don't hold a grudge against my parents for their emotional burdens and mistakes. My heart bled for Edwin's tsuris, and for Judy's. Forgiveness is a gift we give ourselves. Letting go of resentment, anger, and pain liberates our spirits and our minds. Forgiveness is a critical part of emotional healing. That said, I still have more work to do to forgive my siblings for their own abandonment of me, and for their "fucked-upness". The most important message of my story is there is a silver lining beyond my dark cloud. I survived. And I chose to pursue emotional and spiritual healing. We should never give up hope! Each day is an opportunity to heal. An opportunity for growth.

The journey begins with the desire to heal, and the belief that we can achieve spiritual, emotional peace and fulfillment. I don't pretend to know the answers for everyone's problems, but I know what has worked well for me. I believe there is immense value in sharing my story and, hopefully, inspiring others to pursue their own healing. A large, important part of this journey was healing that occurred through art. Painting helped Edwin cope with the pain and suffering of his own tsuris and his blindness. It helped me—and continues to help me—process the complex and painful emotional trauma in my lock box. It is a tool, and a comfort, for which I am profoundly grateful. *(Figures 19-21)*

As part of my grief counseling, my therapists suggested, several times, that I write a final letter to my father, Edwin, to say all the things to him that I always wanted or needed to say to him during our lives. I avoided it for a long time. I didn't feel ready. I hadn't resolved my own heartbreak, and the myriad of feelings toward him well enough to compose such a letter.

Writing this book and the story of my complicated relation-ship with Edwin—the legacy of his abuse and the impact of his inspiration and effect on me—has prepared me to write this letter now. Twenty years of counseling has been the primary foundation of my healing, this includes creating my art. My healing feels more complete, and I feel a sense of closure I've never felt before. Sharing this story of my relationship with my father, Edwin, has been cathartic and has cleansed my soul, spirit, and mind.

I am not perfect; imperfection is a normal part of being human. I still wrestle with my flaws and propensity to bully others, on occasion—an unfortunate and ever-present remnant of my own childhood abuse and dysfunctional family. A remnant that I must perpetually be on guard in my life—and with my family—and must continue to confront it when it occurs.

I am a work in progress—aren't we all. In the hopes that you may find some strength and inspiration for your own healing, I offer my Letter to Edwin to you, as well. Tikkun Olam.

✳✳✳

Daddy,

I have finally fully grown up and have an amazing, beautiful family that I love and cherish with all my heart. I wish you could have known and loved my wife Celeste, and my three children: Alexander, Rachel, and Dana's son Jacob, who we adopted after her passing.

I know you would have loved and adored your grandchildren and would have relished their love for you. I am profoundly sad that you died before my children were born and deeply miss that you never got to meet them, hug them, and play with them.

Thank you for providing me with the treasures which are the foundations for my entire life, my genes, my worldviews, my values, my intellect, my traditions, my religion, my spirituality and faith in God, my work ethic, my unrelenting drive, and my enduring spirit. You inspired my courage, insight, sensitivity, curiosity, creativity, compassion, and strength; you instilled my desire to survive, to heal, and to succeed.

Painting after you became blind crucially inspired me. Your paintings are symbols of your courage, strength, determination, and chutzpah. You defied your disability and never ever gave up hope. Your paintings are a visible symbol of your legacy to me. I am sure you will burst with pride to know that I keep your three beautiful paintings in important visible locations in my home, where I can see them every day. Your paintings remind me of you, your courage, and your legacy, every single day of my life.

Thank you for inspiring me to paint. Painting has been one of your many blessings and gifts to me. Painting has been cathartic and therapeutic; it has fostered my emotional healing and growth, and has allowed me to overcome my own sensitivities, tragedies, and adversity. Painting has opened a new dimension in my life, where my feelings and my subconscious thoughts have an amazing vehicle for vivid expression and release. My art imitates my life; it reflects my anguish, my grief, my heartaches, my pain, and my inner essence. My paintings simply and elegantly express complex feelings and thoughts that cannot be adequately translated into words.

Our paintings vividly symbolize our legacies to our children, our grandchildren, and the world. They serve as a visible enduring symbol of our lives. Our paintings are immortal, even though we are not. The world will not forget us. Our paintings will share our messages and lessons with future generations. Our paintings and our story will hopefully inspire others to seek emotional healing; to overcome addiction, physical, sexual, or emotional abuse, mental illness, adversity, and tragedy. Our message is one of hope; to never give up. Every day is a new opportunity to heal and grow.

I learned profound lessons from your strengths, as well as your imperfections, your abuse, your heartaches, and life tragedies. I am grateful for these diverse, but difficult life lessons. We struggled together through many painful, tragic life lessons; but they have made me stronger, brought me in touch with my feelings, taught me to overcome adversity, and allowed me to survive. Our hard times provided the impetus for me to achieve greatness, to seek help, to gain insight, to release my inner demons, to heal my emotional scars, and to nourish my soul.

I forgive you for your transgressions; the emotional and physical abuse you inflicted on me and our family. I have released my heartache, torment, and pain. I no longer blame you or hold a grudge. I decided not to be a victim, but to be a survivor. I understand how your heartache, intolerable frustration, and frantic anxiety about your impending blindness spurred your abusive behavior; however, I suffered from it, despised it, and vowed adamantly to never perpetuate your abusive behavior within my own family. I kept my promise, but it took a lot of hard work to undo what you taught me. Thank God the chain of abuse has been broken.

My healing has allowed me to become a better parent, husband, friend, physician, and human being. Therapy and painting have allowed me to understand my feelings, decondition my emotional triggers, purge my subconscious irrational fears, and develop healthy coping and communication skills. Therapeutic tools can be readily acquired to greatly enhance our lives and the lives of our families.

I deeply appreciate the memories of the good and bad times we shared together. Our loving, close, beautiful father-son relationship when I was a young child and when we went to college together, are among the best memories of my entire life. It broke my heart when you abused us before you went blind. I felt devastating pain and grief when your Alzheimer's disease ravaged your identity, personality, and intellect at the age of 57. I always wished I could cure your blindness or restore your dissolving brain to normal. Helping you and helping others has been a main motivation in my life. I was frustrated and helpless to fix either problem for you; but frequently prayed to God for a miracle to restore your health, vision, and sanity.

Daddy, I grieve often, with deep feelings for the loss of you, mom, Andy and Dana. Your deaths have impacted me greatly. Your deaths allowed me to learn to intimately embrace my feelings of sadness, anger, and pain. I often feel lonely and sad that I am the sole survivor of our family of origin. I miss you all, despite the fact that you all often drove me crazy. I genuinely love you all and miss you profoundly. Please pass along my message to all our family members in heaven; I think of you often, and eternally love and cherish each of you. I know I will be with you again in heaven someday, but I don't plan on visiting you anytime soon.

Lots of love, Hugs and kisses, Curtis

ABOUT CURTIS DICKMAN

Curtis Dickman resides in Arizona with his wife Celeste, near his three adult children. He has diverse interests, talents, and skills, with insatiable curiosity and immense creativity. He is an accomplished author, artist, student, surgeon, scientist, researcher, inventor, lecturer, educator, and musician.

Curtis is board-certified in neurological surgery; he practiced at the esteemed Barrow Neurological Institute in Phoenix from 1985 until 2015. He is a renowned expert in the surgical treatment of spinal disorders. He was senior editor of the journal *SPINE*, wrote and edited multiple neurosurgical textbooks, and published over 160 peer reviewed scientific articles in medical journals.

Curtis is a passionate artist; his emotionally laden, innovative artwork often incorporates painting, sculpture, digital art, photography, and optical illusions.

More information about Curtis's artwork and stories is available at www.curtisdickman.com and www.CurtisDickmanFineArt.com.

Curtis is devoted to multiple charities, particularly those which aid abused children. He serves on the Board of CHILDHELP, a nonprofit organization whose programs directly serve abused children and their families, focusing on meeting the children's physical, emotional, educational and spiritual needs.

Proceeds from the sale of this book will be donated to charities devoted to abused children and PTSD recovery.

AUTHORS COMMENTS:

Advances in neuroscience and behavioral medicine have allowed us to better understand, target and treat the specific brain areas responsible for post-traumatic stress disorder (PTSD). Noninvasive, nonsurgical techniques (like EMDR and brain spotting, referenced below) access the brain circuitry responsible for triggering and sustaining traumatic memories. These brain regions can be effectively accessed, and the traumatic emotional memories desensitized to reduce or eliminate the impact of PTSD triggers. PTSD can occur at any age, to any person. It is not solely confined to war veterans or victims of child abuse.

There are many promising new methods for effectively treating PTSD, which are beyond the scope of this book to discuss in detail here.(See recommended reading)

Extensive clinical research has defined the pivotal role of adverse childhood experiences (ACEs) in predicting major medical and psychological disorders during life. ACEs are episodes of childhood neglect, deprivation, assault, physical, sexual, or emotional abuse which are associated with childhood PTSD. ACEs (or adult PTSD) can accumulate and predispose individuals to serious illnesses, addictions, and dysfunction unless the contents of the brains protective memory circuitry are effectively treated.

The personal, social, and financial costs of ACEs and PTSD are staggering. They are associated with high rates of addiction, divorce, suicide, psychiatric disease, physical disease, disability, and premature death.

RESOURCES

Childhelp National Child Abuse Hotline Resources: https://childhelphotline.org/

Children's Resources: Children's Resources - Childhelp

Parent Resources: Parent's Resources - Childhelp

Educator Resources: Educator's Resources - Childhelp

NATIONAL CENTER FOR PTSD.   https://www.ptsd.va.gov/

https://www.cdc.gov/violenceprevention/aces/index.html

http://www.pacesconnection.com/

http://acestoohigh.com

http://developingchild.harvard.edu/science/key-concepts/toxic-stress/

http://childtrauma.org/

RECOMMENDED READING:

What Happened To You? Conversations on Trauma, Resilience and Healing. Oprah Winfrey and Bruce D Perry MD PhD Flatiron Books . 2021.

When The Body Says No. Understanding the Stress-Disease Connection. Gabor Mate MD

The Murray Method: Creating Wholeness Beyond Trauma, Abuse, Neglect and Addiction
by Marilyn Murray | Feb 1, 2021

Prisoner of Another War: A Remarkable Journey of Healing from Childhood Trauma
by Marilyn Murray | Sep 1, 1991

Complex PTSD Workbook: A Mind-Body Approach To Regaining Emotional Control And Becoming Whole
by Arielle Schwartz

The Body Keeps the Score: Brain, Mind, and Body in the Healing of Trauma
by Bessel van der Kolk M.D. | Sep 8, 2015

Brainspotting: The Revolutionary New Therapy for Rapid and Effective Change
by David Grand PhD, Jonathan Todd Ross, et al.

Transforming The Living Legacy of Trauma: A Workbook for Survivors and Therapists Paperback –
February 1, 2021 by Janina Fisher

A Practical Guide to Complex PTSD: Compassionate Strategies to Begin Healing from Childhood Trauma
by Arielle Schwartz PhD

EMDR Toolbox: Theory and Treatment of Complex PTSD and Dissociation: Theory and Treatment of Complex PTSD and Dissociation (Second Edition, Paperback) – Highly Rated EMDR Book by James Knipe PhD | Sep 28, 2018

Mental Health: 6 Books in 1 - *The Attachment Theory, Abandonment Anxiety, Depression in Relationships, Addiction Recovery, Complex PTSD, Trauma, CBT, EMDR Therapy and Somatic Psychotherapy*

PTSD & EMDR WORKBOOK 2 books in 1: *Self-Help Techniques for Overcoming Traumatic Stress Symptoms Thanks To The Eye Movement Desensitization And Reprocessing (Emdr) Therapy*
by Anthony Russel | Nov 13, 2019

In An Unspoken Voice. How the Body Releases Trauma and Restores Goodness.
By Peter A Levine, PhD. | North Atlantic Books, 2010

DBT Skills Training Manual. Second Edition
By Marsha M Linehan |The Guilford Press. 2015

DBT Skills Training. Handouts And Worksheets. Second Edition
By Marsha M Linehan |The Guilford Press. 2015